KASKASKIA

KASKASKIA

THE LOST CAPITAL OF ILLINOIS

DAVID MACDONALD
AND RAINE WATERS

Southern Illinois University Press
Carbondale

Southern Illinois University Press
www.siupress.com

Cover illustration: *top*, View of Kaskaskia, engraving from J. Meyer, *Meyer's Universum*, 18 (Hildburghausen: Verlag des Bibliographischen Instituts, 1857), following p. 156; *bottom*, earthworks of Fort Kaskaskia, photograph by MacDonald and Waters, spring 2015.

Library of Congress Cataloging-in-Publication Data
Names: MacDonald, David, 1943– author. | Waters, Raine, author.
Title: Kaskaskia : the lost capital of Illinois / David MacDonald and Raine Waters.
Description: Carbondale : Southern Illinois University Press, 2019. | Series: Shawnee books | Includes bibliographical references and index.
Identifiers: LCCN 2018041357 | ISBN 9780809337316 (paperback) | ISBN 9780809337323 (ebook)
Subjects: LCSH: Kaskaskia (Ill.)—History. | BISAC: HISTORY / United States / State & Local / Midwest (IA, IL, IN, KS, MI, MN, MO, ND, NE, OH, SD, WI). | SOCIAL SCIENCE / Regional Studies. | HISTORY / Social History. | ARCHITECTURE / Regional.
Classification: LCC F549.K3 M28 2019 | DDC 977.3/92—dc23 LC record available at https://lccn.loc.gov/2018041357

CONTENTS

FIGURES

vii

ACKNOWLEDGMENTS

OUR THANKS TO Margaret K. Brown and Emily Lyons, fountainheads of knowledge and aid. Carl Ekberg, as ever, is a source of information, insight, and critical acumen. We thank Judge Morris Arnold, David Ramsey, and Robert Mueller for their constant encouragement and good humor.

KASKASKIA

INTRODUCTION

THERE ARE MANY types of history. Much modern history is thesis-driven, the mustering of facts and examples to demonstrate a particular interpretation of the past. This sort of history necessarily interposes the author's understanding between the sources and the reader. Another type is descriptive, presenting material to the reader with minimal interpretation to enable the reader to see and interpret the past for him- or herself. That is the sort of history we have endeavored to write here, a simple exposition of Kaskaskia, the largest town in Illinois from the time of its founding in 1703 until well into the nineteenth century.

Colonial Kaskaskia was a center of French culture and language in Illinois and the largest of the French villages in Illinois, a prosperous agricultural settlement exporting grain and other resources down the Mississippi to Louisiana. The return trip brought the goods of Europe to the middle of the wilderness, where the citizens of Kaskaskia enjoyed a lifestyle far more sophisticated than that of the pioneers slowly advancing the frontier from the Eastern Seaboard. Life in French Kaskaskia, of course, was not without problems. War came near at times and claimed the lives of local citizens, and crops did not thrive every year. Still, for two generations the inhabitants of Kaskaskia were prosperous and content, but that happy state ended suddenly.

The French government lost Canada and then abandoned Illinois and Louisiana at the end of the French and Indian War. The town suffered through more than a decade of inept and corrupt British rule that drove many citizens across the Mississippi to the Spanish-ruled west bank.

During the American Revolution, George Rogers Clark captured the town from the British, securing Illinois for the United States. The emerging nation, however, could not adequately govern the new territory, and during the 1780s, the citizens of Kaskaskia lived through an era of virtual anarchy, during which they lived in fear or abandoned their homes and fled. A priest lamented Kaskaskia's situation, and from that lament arose the first notion that Kaskaskia suffered under a curse.

Kaskaskia did revive when the United States was finally able to assert control in the 1790s. Kaskaskia became the capital of the Illinois Territory and then the first state capital of Illinois, and the town was home to leading political and economic figures in the early, shaping years of Illinois. Good fortune, however, did not long endure. Natural disasters of unprecedented magnitude—crop failure, earthquake, tornado, flood, and pestilence—seemed to haunt Kaskaskia and robbed the town of vitality. People came to regard Kaskaskia, once the center and focus of Illinois, as just a quaint and somehow foreign relic. Finally, the great river, so long Kaskaskia's highway and source of its prosperity, turned on the town, washing away the buildings and even the very ground on which it was built. The changing course of the Mississippi was merely the coup de grâce, the finishing blow, the last of the disasters that led even reasonable people to wonder whether Kaskaskia had been cursed. As the last of old Kaskaskia fell victim to the river, newspaper reporters, eager to fill pages with sensational stories, seized on old notions and combined them with their own creative imaginations to present new fictions as old traditions. Some still regard these late fictions seriously. Others less credulous reject this fake lore but still feel that an aura of the unnatural surrounds the events that befell Kaskaskia and led to its final destruction.

Today, new Kaskaskia, now a tiny village with fewer than a score of inhabitants a few miles from the location of the old town, preserves some of the relics of old Kaskaskia. The furnishings of the church date to the early days of the French town, and visitors can see the bell sent by the king of France to Kaskaskia in 1741 and rung to announce George Rogers Clark's annexation of Illinois to the United States. New Kaskaskia is well worth a visit, but it is nothing like the old town.

Other relics of old Kaskaskia also survive: written documents, objects, maps, engravings, sketches, and photographs made before the city crumbled into the Mississippi River. (We exclude all imagined reconstructions; the only modern illustrations are photographs of objects that still exist.) They all contain some essence of the lost town so important to the origin of modern Illinois and perhaps also some of the atmosphere that led people to whisper that Kaskaskia had fallen under a curse.

PART 1

HISTORY OF KASKASKIA

CHAPTER 1

DAWN OF KASKASKIA, 1673–1719

MISSIONARIES AND INDIANS

THE EVENTS THAT led to the founding of Kaskaskia began decades earlier in an Indian village along the Illinois River just about opposite modern Starved Rock. The villagers were mainly of the Kaskaskia tribe, along with some Peoria and Miami. The Kaskaskia, Peoria, Cahokia, Michigamea, and a number of small tribes, such as the Tamaroa, formed the Illinois, an alliance of tribes sharing language and culture and frequently intermarrying. The Miami were also closely related to the Illinois and were often but not consistently allied with them. In 1673, the Jesuit missionary Father Claude Allouez came to this village, where he stayed about two months. In 1677, Father Allouez officially became head of the mission to the Kaskaskia, visiting the Kaskaskia, Peoria, and Miami in various villages and during their annual hunts, until his death in 1689.

In 1680, the Iroquois brutally ravaged the Kaskaskia village, killing many. In 1691, the Kaskaskia, motivated by fear of Iroquois raids, the hostility of the Fox to the north, and the depletion of resources in the vicinity of their old village, moved southward along the Illinois River to Pimiteoui (modern Peoria), where they settled with the Peoria. After the death of Father Allouez, Father Jacques Gravier administered the mission to the Kaskaskia and made a significant number of conversions.

In 1700, the Kaskaskia, still threatened by the Iroquois and even more by the growing hostility of the Fox, moved south again, accompanied by Fathers Gravier and Marest. They settled on the western bank of the Mississippi along the small Des Peres River, in the southern part of modern

St. Louis, where many of the Tamaroa joined them. It was probably fear
of the Sioux that led the Kaskaskia to abandon their village at the Des
Peres River early in the spring of 1703 and travel about sixty miles south to
settle by the Michigamea, another Illinois tribe, on the bank of what was
then known as the Michigamea River, later renamed the Kaskaskia River,
at the southern end of what came to be called the American Bottom.[1]

The American Bottom consists of the Mississippi River floodplain on
the eastern side of the Mississippi River, extending from the confluence
of the Illinois and Mississippi Rivers in the north to the mouth of the Kaskaskia River in the south. The northern section from Alton to Cahokia
is in places narrowly confined by limestone bluffs. The French did not
settle there. The section south of Cahokia, extending about sixty miles,
is fertile and moist. Away from the river, bluffs border the American
Bottom, varying from steep hills to sheer cliffs well over a hundred feet
high. A few streams have carved ravines through the bluffs. The width
of the bottomland between river and bluffs varies greatly but generally
is at least several miles.

Kaskaskia was only one among five French villages established in the
American Bottom in the last years of the seventeenth century through
the first decades of the eighteenth: Cahokia, St. Philippe, Chartres, Prairie
du Rocher, and Kaskaskia (fig. 1.1). They were not planned settlements but
rather grew spontaneously, unlike the majority of other French colonial
towns, such as New Orleans, that royal officials laid out in an orderly
manner. French missionaries, fur traders, and farmers lived in proximity
to the Illinois Indians, who inhabited their own villages. In the eighteenth
century, the French also established Ste. Geneviève, on the western bank
of the Mississippi, and outlying settlements at Vincennes on the Wabash
River and Peoria on the Illinois River. Collectively, the area of all of these
settlements was known as *le pays des Illinois*, the Illinois Country.

KASKASKIA, 1703–1719

THE KASKASKIA SETTLED on the southern bank of a river that came to
be called by their name, about six miles from its confluence with the
Mississippi, along with Jesuit missionaries and a few French traders who
had married Kaskaskia women. Land for farm or pasture was excellent
and abundant, and soon some of the traders settled down to become
resident farmers. The Kaskaskia River offered a safer anchorage than

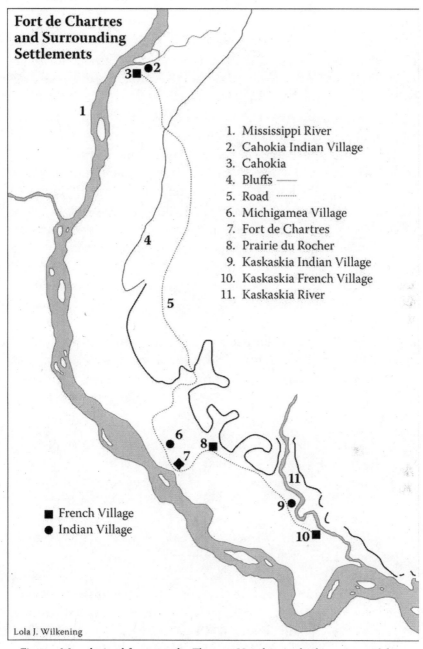

Fort de Chartres and Surrounding Settlements

1. Mississippi River
2. Cahokia Indian Village
3. Cahokia
4. Bluffs ——
5. Road ········
6. Michigamea Village
7. Fort de Chartres
8. Prairie du Rocher
9. Kaskaskia Indian Village
10. Kaskaskia French Village
11. Kaskaskia River

■ French Village
● Indian Village

Lola J. Wilkening

Fig. 1.1. Map derived from one by Thomas Hutchins, which was copied from an anonymous French manuscript map of the 1760s now in the Archives centrales de la Marine at the Château de Vincennes in Paris. Hutchins, *A Plan of the Several Villages in the Illinois Country with Part of the River Mississippi &c.*, in *A Topographical Description of Virginia, Pennsylvania, Maryland, and North Carolina* (London: printed for the author and sold by J. Almon, 1778).

the swift-flowing Mississippi, and the Kaskaskia had convenient access to the Ohio and Wabash Rivers and the trade they carried. Voyageurs carrying material to and from Canada or the Gulf Coast frequently visited the community.[2]

From its founding until 1717, the French colonial government in Canada officially administered the Illinois Country, but Canada was far away, communications slow, and the settlements in Illinois small and of little importance. The French colony in Louisiana, founded in 1699, was frequently in a better position to respond to problems in Illinois. So in 1711, the governor of Louisiana dispatched a small group of troops up the Mississippi to deal with French Canadian traders who, according Jesuit complaints, were debauching the Native American women and hampering missionary activities. Along with the troops was André Pénicaut, a naval carpenter from La Rochelle in France, who claims to have been involved at least peripherally in virtually all of the important events in Louisiana from his arrival about 1699 until his return to France in 1721, after which he published an account of his time in America. In 1711, Kaskaskia was an Indian village where a few French also resided, and Pénicaut was much more concerned with describing the Kaskaskia Indians' absorption of French culture than describing the physical appearance of the settlement:[3]

> The Cascassias Illinois are hard-working and skillful in tilling the fields. They plow them with a plow, which has not yet been done elsewhere in all the Lower Missicipy. They acquired a knowledge of the plow from the Reverend Jesuit Fathers more than sixty years ago, as early as the time they were residing near Lake Pinthouy.[4] The Reverend Jesuit Fathers had come there by way of Canada to get down to these Illinois and had converted almost all of them to the Catholic religion.[5]
>
> The region in which they are presently settled is one of the finest in all Louisiana and one of the best for fertility of the soil. Wheat grows there as fine as any in France, and all kinds of vegetables, roots, and grasses. Also, they have all kinds of fruits, of an excellent taste. It is among the Illinois that one finds the most beautiful prairies along the bank of the Missicipy; here they graze horses which they buy from the Cadodaquioux[6] in exchange for merchandise. On these prairies, too, they have a great deal of livestock, such as bullocks, cows, etc. Also

at their settlement are many fowl of every kind; and, moreover, they
have fishing in the stream, and in the Missicipy River two leagues
from their village, where they catch a great many fish; so they do not
lack any of the necessities and comforts of life.

Near their village they have three mills to grind their grains: namely,
one windmill belonging to the Reverend Jesuit Fathers, which is used
quite often by the residents, and two others, horse mills, owned by
the Illinois themselves. . . .

The majority of the Illinois are Catholic Christians. They have
in their village a rather large church in which there is a baptismal
font. This church is quite clean on the inside. There are three chapels, the main one of the choir and two side chapels. They have a
belltower, with a bell. They attend high Mass and Vespers quite
regularly. The Reverend Jesuit Fathers have translated the Psalms
and the hymns from Latin to their language. At Mass or Vespers
the Illinois sing one stanza of the Psalm or hymn in their language,
and the French the following stanza in Latin, and so on with the
remaining ones, and in the key in which they are sung in Europe
among Catholic Christians.

The mission church Pénicaut describes was one the Jesuits had erected
in 1703, the year the settlement was founded. No contemporary illustration of it survives, but it seems to have been built in the *poteaux en terre*
technique, in which vertical logs were planted in a trench, and roofed
with thatched straw. The church served Kaskaskia for about thirty years.[7]

From its founding in 1699 until 1714, Louisiana was a royal colony. In
1714, the king granted control to a proprietor, who controlled the colony economically while conforming to royal policies. Several successive
proprietors hoped to make a profit from the colony, but earnings were
disappointing. In 1717, the king transferred the administration of Illinois
from Canada to Louisiana. This remained a contentious issue between
the two colonies throughout the French regime. In 1718, the governor of
Louisiana, Jean-Baptiste Le Moyne de Bienville, appointed Pierre-Sidrac
Dugué de Boisbriand commandant of the Illinois Country. He arrived in
Kaskaskia the next year to establish a fort to house the marines and serve
as a military and administrative center. Boisbriand chose a site about
eighteen miles north of Kaskaskia and forty miles south of Cahokia,
where he had the first Fort de Chartres built, 1719–1720. Kaskaskia, at the

southern end of the American Bottom, was poorly located for a military center for the entire region, but a contingent of troops was regularly stationed there. The troops were apparently welcomed by the population, and although individual marines sometimes engaged in troublesome behavior, there was never significant antagonism between the town and the troops during the French period.

THE SEPARATION OF INDIAN KASKASKIA

In 1719, Pierre-Sidrac Dugué de Boisbriand, commandant of the Illinois Country, separated the Kaskaskia Indians from French Kaskaskia. The Kaskaskia established their own village along with the Michigamea several miles up the Kaskaskia River from the French settlement.[8] Within a few years, the Michigamea moved to their own separate village near Fort de Chartres. The sources do not make it clear whether the Michigamea or the French instituted that movement.

Boisbriand had good reasons to separate the Indian and French communities, and there is no indication that the Kaskaskia opposed it. Despite the generally good relations between the Kaskaskia and French, cultural differences sometimes led to quarrels. For example, tribesmen sometimes hunted the French farmers' free-ranging livestock as though they were wild animals. Separation made such frictions less likely to lead to violence and allowed opportunities for the Jesuit missionaries to intervene and maintain the peace. The Jesuits were also concerned about the corrupting influence of the French voyageurs and traders, whom they denounced for debauching the native women and promoting drunkenness among the men, which frequently led to violence.

Despite the official separation of communities, the people of Indian Kaskaskia and French Kaskaskia remained close. (Figure 1.2 is a French representation of Indians from several nations.) Members of both communities often traveled the few miles between the two, and marriages between French men and Illinois women were common, particularly in the early eighteenth century. Officials at the highest level disapproved and even officially prohibited intermarriages, but the Jesuits continued to sanction them. Ordinarily, Indian brides were thoroughly absorbed into the French community.[9]

When Boisbriand divided the French and the Kaskaskia Indians into separate communities, the Jesuits moved their mission to Indian

Fig. 1.2. *Desseins de sauvages de plusieurs nations, New Orleans, 1735,* a colored pen-and-ink sketch by Alexandre de Batz. The writing on the image labels the standing Indian at the right "Atakapas," the black child "Negre," the seated woman at the left "Renarde sauvagese Esclave," the squatting man with the painted face "Dansseur," and the central group "Illinois Sauvagesse." Courtesy of the Peabody Museum of Archaeology and Ethnology, Harvard University, PM#41–72–10/20; gift of the Estate of Belle J. Bushnell, 1941.

Kaskaskia, where they erected a new church and parochial residence. The Jesuits also continued to minister to French Kaskaskia, where they maintained their headquarters. The baptismal register reflects the change, bearing the new heading "Registre des Baptêmes fait dans l'église de la Mission et dans la Paroisse de la Conception" (Register of Baptisms performed in the church of the Mission and in the Parish of the Conception).[10]

In that same year, 1719, a French officer, Bernard Diron d'Artaguiette, surveyed the Mississippi from New Orleans to Cahokia, and his observations were eventually turned into a map printed in 1732. A detail from the map shows the spatial relation of the French and Native American settlements (fig. 1.3).

Sieur Malic was, to use the better attested form of his name, Pierre Melique, a lieutenant of the marines and part of the Illinois garrison. He came to Fort de Chartres at the time of its establishment in 1719, and he built a considerable establishment on the road between Indian and French Kaskaskias, including at least four houses.[11]

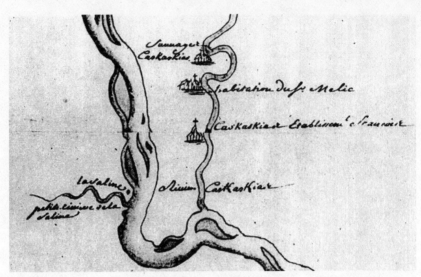

Fig. 1.3. Detail from *Fleuve S\`. Louis cy devant Mississipy Relevé a la Boussolle par le S\`. Diron L'an 1719 depuis la Nouvelle Orleans en montant jusqu'au village Sauvage Cahokiá Païs des Illinois distance de 230 lieües en ligne directe, et de 400 lieües Suivant les circuits et les detours. A Paris le 19e may 1732.* The labels on the right half of the map, from the north (*top*) to the south, are *Sauvages Caskaskias*, Native Kaskaskia; *habitation de Sr. Malic*, residence of Sieur Malic; *Caskaskias Etablissemen\` Français*, French Kaskaskia Settlement; and *Rivière Caskaskias*, Kaskaskia River. On the left, the labels are *La Saline*, the saltworks, and *petite rivière de la Saline*, Little Saline River. Original Paris, BSH, C 4040–13. Published in W. C. Temple, *Indian Villages of the Illinois Country*, part 1, Atlas Supplement (Springfield: Illinois State Museum, 1975), plate XVI. Courtesy of the Abraham Lincoln Presidential Library and Museum.

CHAPTER 2

FRENCH AND INDIAN
KASKASKIAS, 1719–1765

AS THE EIGHTEENTH century progressed, Kaskaskia grew slowly, and the population of Kaskaskia and the Illinois Country as a whole remained small. In late 1722 and early 1723, Bernard Diron d'Artaguiette, who had surveyed the Mississippi in 1719, again traveled upriver from New Orleans, this time as the inspector general of Louisiana, conducting a census on his way (fig. 2.1). French censuses were infrequent and never completely accurate and comprehensive, but they suffice to give some idea of the community. At Kaskaskia, Diron recorded 64 *habitants* (land-owning settlers), 41 French laborers, 37 women, and 54 children, for a total of 196. Diron did not count black and Indian slaves, free Indians living in tribal villages, garrison troops, or transient hunters, traders, and voyageurs. Although small, Kaskaskia was the largest of the French settlements in the Illinois Country.[1]

Diron kept a journal during his inspection tour, a valuable historical document for early Louisiana and the Illinois Country.[2] He provided a description of Kaskaskia written just twenty years after its founding and four years after the separation of the French and Indian communities:

Apr. 17 (1723). At midday we arrived at the entrance of the *Petite Riviere des Cascakias*,[3] which is on the right as you ascend. It is two leagues up this river on the left (on the right is a border of high mountains) in a vast prairie that is situated the French village called the Cascakias, which is composed entirely of farmers who live there

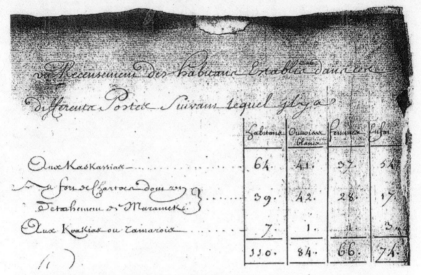

Fig. 2.1. Portion of the Diron d'Artaguiette census of 1723 reporting the population of Kaskaskia, Chartres and vicinity, and Cahokia. Few French manuscripts of the period are written in such a clear, elegant hand. ANC C13A.8.226v. Photograph courtesy of Carl Ekberg.

very comfortably. French wheat grows very well there and of a fine quality, of which they gather a fairly large quantity, which they sell for the subsistence of the troops. All the other vegetables necessary to life grow very well there. Their houses are all built of frame timbers on the ground. The chimneys are of stone, of which they could very easily build their entire houses, as the stone there is of very good quality and ready at hand, but the scarcity of men has prevented them from undertaking this work. Several inhabitants also have horse tread mills of their own with which they grind their French wheat. There is also a church there, which is certainly the finest in the colony. This church is ministered to by a Jesuit who performs the functions of curate and takes the tithes which are fairly large.

There is in this village a windmill made of wood, belonging to the Reverend Jesuit Fathers. It was formerly placed on the bank of the Petite Riviere, but as it got little wind in this place, they considered it wise to place it in the middle of the prairie, upon their own land, where it is certainly better off. The Jesuit priests have a little farm in this place, which they manage themselves. I do not give here the number of their cattle nor their other property, because I have put it in a general enumeration which will be found affixed hereto.[4] It is six leagues by land and twelve by water from this village to Fort de Chartres. A league higher up on the same side on the road which leads to Fort de Chartres and upon the same river is found the settlement of Sr. Melicq, lieutenant of the company of Artaguiette, which he manages himself. They gather here French wheat, maize, beans, peas, pumpkins and other vegetables. From this place, continuing along the road to Fort de Chartres, at the upper end of the same prairie as that upon which Sr. Melicq is, a half league higher up on the bank of the same river, is the Indian village of the Ilinnois, who number about 200 warriors. From this village one goes on through beautiful wide prairies which are cut only by a few fringes of timber, to the above-mentioned Fort de Chartres.

The Fox Indians had been the enemies of the Illinois tribes even before the Illinois came into contact with the French, and virtually every year during the 1720s, the Fox raided boldly into Illinois Country, attacking and killing Illinois and French alike. The Illinois were often unable to defend themselves or retaliate effectively. Fox attacks grew so severe that both French and Indians fled from the smaller villages to Kaskaskia, but the Fox penetrated even into the outskirts there. In early spring 1725, the Fox killed two citizens of Kaskaskia, one of them a prominent churchwarden, "deux pas" (two steps) from the town.[5] Pierre Melique (the more common spelling of the name), mentioned in Diron's journal, had developed a profitable estate between French and Indian Kaskaskias, but in 1727 the Fox killed him and seven other men on their way to the Missouri post.[6] That same year Commandant Pierre-Charles Desliette moved most of the garrison from Fort de Chartres to Kaskaskia. A flood had badly damaged the fort, and after relocation he could better protect the inhabitants at Kaskaskia. Despite frequent complaints from Illinois and New Orleans, the Canadian administration, resentful that Illinois had been transferred to Louisiana, did little to relieve the situation until Paris sent a new governor to Canada charged with ending the Fox wars. In 1730, combined French forces and Indians of many tribes, including marines, militiamen, and Indians from Illinois, almost wiped out the Fox, but the Fox reemerged several decades later to bedevil the Illinois again.

In 1731, the royal government resumed direct control of Louisiana from the failed administration of proprietors, the Compagnie des Indes,

and ordered a new census. The Illinois section, dated January 1, 1732, lists
the population of Kaskaskia as 352. Little more than half of the inhabitants of Kaskaskia were French, of French descent, or Indian women who
had married French men and become part of the French community.
Almost half of the population were slaves. Adult black slaves slightly
outnumbered adult Indian slaves. The census listed black children but
no Indian children. Children of Indian mothers married to French men
were always counted as legitimate children; others of unwed mothers fell
into the category of illegitimate children and orphans. Over half of the
people in the Illinois Country, excluding Indians living in tribal villages
and the transient population, lived in Kaskaskia.[7]

In addition to those recorded in the census, there were others who
only visited Kaskaskia intermittently. Voyageurs used Kaskaskia as a
convenient base, coming and going throughout the year. Indians, both
Illinois and other tribes, and French hunters and traders visited Kaskaskia seasonally, bartering horses, bear oil, tallow, salted buffalo flanks
and tongues, furs, and hides for European goods. Deer hides were of
greatest importance, but shipments downriver included the skins of
virtually every fur-bearing animal in the region. In addition to these
products, the farmers of Kaskaskia and the other Illinois villages were
able in most years to send many tons of wheat flour downriver to feed
southern Louisiana, where wheat did not grow. Onions, dried peas, wild
ginseng, and hams, both pork and bear, were also exported from Illinois
in quantity. Salt too was an important commodity, extracted from the
salt springs on Saline Creek across the Mississippi near Kaskaskia. The
French produced quantities of lead from the abundant ore deposits in
Missouri near Kaskaskia, but labor was scarce, transportation costs high,
and profits low. Men mined lead in small-scale digs when not engaged
in agricultural work.[8]

Agriculture at Kaskaskia was similar to that of other French villages
in Illinois and elsewhere. Farmers owned and cultivated long narrow
lots in a large agricultural area that they fenced and maintained collectively. French officials originally conveyed ownership to these lots
by land grant, and subsequently lots could be bought, bartered, or sold.
Some lots fronted on both the Kaskaskia and Mississippi Rivers, others
just on the Mississippi. The long lots minimized the number of turns
the plowman had to make. The southern part of the peninsula between
the two rivers was held in common by the community and was used as

pasture. The commons were formally established around the time French Kaskaskia became a separate community in 1719 and confirmed by a royal French patent in 1743. The British confirmed the rights of the citizens of Kaskaskia to the commons in 1763, and the United States did the same in 1810. The Kaskaskia commons ceased to exist in the early twentieth century when the state supervised the sale of the land.[9]

Official convoys of *bateaux*, boats of varying designs, and *pirogues*, dugout canoes, some very large, carried goods up and down the river, normally one convoy in the spring and another in the fall. Private bateaux and pirogues often joined the official convoys and sometimes journeyed alone. In time of war, convoys were sometimes canceled. In the mid-1730s, the hostile Chickasaw virtually closed the Mississippi for two years. In addition to the official convoys to and from New Orleans, other convoys carrying trade spread out across the network of rivers and portages that served as highways for the French in America.[10]

No sooner had the Fox menace abated than a new threat appeared, the English-allied Chickasaw. Although the Chickasaw were a small tribe, they were intrepid fighters and were protected by the remoteness of their homeland. In the 1730s, Jean-Baptiste Le Moyne de Bienville, governor of Louisiana, twice showed himself inept at planning and executing campaigns against the Chickasaw. The Fort de Chartres marines and the local militias from Kaskaskia and the other French villages were fully involved in these campaigns and suffered many casualties. Eventually the parties made a peace treaty of sorts, but incidents and outbreaks of violence continued long afterward.

In 1738, the French authorities felt that the Chickasaw threat to Kaskaskia warranted the construction of a fort on the bluff across the Kaskaskia River to defend the town. The commandant had stone quarried for the fort, but before much else could be done, expenses mounted far beyond original estimates, and to the south Bienville's futile campaigns against the Chickasaw were staggeringly costly. The royal government canceled construction of the fort, but the building materials did not go to waste. The old village log church, built in 1703, had deteriorated, and in 1737 the villagers had begun to build a new church. Father Tartarin, and the *marguilliers*, elected lay churchwardens responsible for the administration of church property, asked for the stone cut for the fort to build the church. Governor Bienville and Edmé Gatien de Salmon, chief financial officer for the colony, wrote to the royal government supporting the request, adding that, unless the stone were guarded carefully, people would simply pilfer it. The government minister replied that the stone could be used for the church but that Salmon should sell it to the parish for the best price he could get.[11] It is doubtful that the royal treasury recovered much from the sale. The new church, built largely from the stone originally destined for the fort, was completed in 1740. The cornerstone survives (fig. 2.2).

Many accounts of early Kaskaskia claim mistakenly that the stone church was built in 1714 rather than 1740. A memoir written by Father Benedict Roux, pastor of Kaskaskia from 1835 to 1839, is the original source for this error. Father Roux's memoir was not published fully until 1918, but an anonymous author, probably Roux himself, relied heavily on it in an article published in 1845, which spread the story.[12] Where Roux based part of his account of early Kaskaskia on parish records, it is valuable and accurate, but Roux also derived much material from interviews with elderly inhabitants whom he called "the Ancients of Kaskaskia." His naïve faith in the accuracy of oral history led him into many errors. For example, he wrote that Fort Kaskaskia was built in 1712; it was actually begun in 1738 and never finished during the French era. He claimed the Jesuits withdrew from Kaskaskia in 1765 because of the hostility of the

Fig. 2.2. Cornerstone of the Church of the Immaculate Conception begun in 1737, completed in 1740, now imbedded in the wall of the Kaskaskia Bell State Memorial, Kaskaskia. Photograph by MacDonald and Waters.

British, but actually they were expelled by the French government in 1763. Roux also dated the American capture of Kaskaskia to 1783 rather than the correct year of 1778. Substituting 1714 for the correct date of the church's construction, 1740, is an error of a sort commonly encountered in oral traditions. The two dates sound alike, for one, and oral accounts often exaggerate the antiquity of events, for another.

The Kaskaskia Manuscripts, a collection of over six thousand documents, are of inestimable importance for the study of Kaskaskia and all of French Illinois. The bulk of the documents from the French regime come from the period between 1720 and 1765. The great majority of the Kaskaskia documents are notarial records, such as property sales, leases, wills, postmortem inventories, marriage contracts, partnerships, labor contracts, acknowledgments of debt, and records of payments. No document was legal until it had been recorded by the notary, who prepared a copy for each of the parties and retained one for his records. The notary often served also as the clerk of court, and sometimes the records of the clerk of the court were included in the notarial files. The documents offer a rich, textured record of society at Kaskaskia and the other French towns.

Early Kaskaskia was home to notable people, and details of their lives are often to be found in the Kaskaskia Manuscripts. Marie Rouensa-8cate8a is one of the most famous, largely due to the research of C. J. Ekberg and A. J. Pregaldin.[13] The 8 symbol in her name indicates a phoneme approximating *ou*. Jesuit Father Jacques Gravier's dramatic and almost theatrical account is the primary source for her early life, conversion, subsequent conflict with her father, and marriage; the Kaskaskia Manuscripts provide information about her later life and death. 8cate8a, to use her original name, was the daughter of the major chief of the Kaskaskia, Rouensa. About 1694, while the tribe was living at Pimiteoui (modern Peoria), Father Gravier converted 8cate8a to Christianity and baptized her as Marie Rouensa. Gravier had previously made over two hundred conversions in the tribe, but in contrast to Marie, most were infants, the elderly on their deathbeds, or young women of no particular influence. Marie, about eighteen years old, wished to remain unmarried and to devote her life to Christ, but her father wanted her to marry a French trader, Michel Accault, forty-eight years old and notorious for his debaucheries. Such a marriage would secure a favorable trade relation with the French. Rouensa attempted to force Marie into marriage and even threatened Father Gravier's missionary work, but initially Marie resisted resolutely, though torn between her ideal of a religious life and her duty to obey her father.

After consulting with Father Gravier, Marie finally agreed to marry Accault, provided that he reform, her parents convert to Christianity, and Gravier's work go on without interference. Subsequently the Kaskaskia converted to Christianity in increasing numbers, although it would be years before all the tribe accepted the religion. Marie and Accault had two sons before his death, about 1702, and like most women of her time, Marie did not remain a widow long and married another French trader, Michel Philippe.

After the Kaskaskia moved to the southern end of the American Bottom along with Jesuit missionaries and French traders who had married into the tribe, Philippe became a major figure—a successful farmer, landowner, and militia officer—and Marie bore him six children, three sons and three daughters. When the Kaskaskia Indians separated from the French in 1719, Marie remained in French Kaskaskia. Indian women who married French men usually became thoroughly integrated into the French community. Marie died in 1725, her estate distributed according to the principles of French law. Her will and a codicil are preserved among the Kaskaskia Manuscripts, written in French. Father Jean-Baptiste Le Boullenger conferred with Marie to compose the will and put it into proper form, and then it was read twice to Marie in the Kaskaskian language. In more than thirty years Marie must have acquired some French, but perhaps when confronted with legal complexities, she felt more confident in her native language. One concern darkened her last days. Her daughters all married well, and her sons with one exception had joined the French society of Illinois without a problem; but her second son, Michel Accault *fils*, abandoned the French community and went to live with the Indians, where he married an unconverted Indian woman without the sanction of the church. Marie disinherited him unless he repented and returned. Upon her death Marie Rouensa received a unique honor of burial under the floor of the parish church of Kaskaskia, the only women so honored.

Some high officials opposed marriages between French and Indians, but the Jesuits held no such reservations and sanctified such marriages despite royal disapproval so long as both partners were Catholic. Marriage between Frenchmen and Indians was common at all levels of society in Illinois. Louis Turpin was one of the most prominent men of early

Kaskaskia. Born in Montréal in 1694, he settled in Kaskaskia, where he became a large landowner, a wealthy merchant, and captain of the militia. His three-story home was the largest in Kaskaskia. Turpin married three times. His second wife, Dorothée Mechipe8ta, was an Indian, and his daughter Marie entered the Ursaline convent in New Orleans, the only Illinois woman to do so.

Jacques Bourdon was also one of the wealthiest men in the village, and he too became captain of the militia, as well as serving as de facto royal notary. He had eight children by one or perhaps two Indian wives—the records are not clear on that point.[14] Many of the French settlers of early Kaskaskia married Indian women, but as the years passed, marriages between the French and Indians declined, owing both to an increase in the French population and to a sharp decline in the Illinois Indian population.

The Kaskaskia Manuscripts were initially kept at Fort de Chartres and in the office of the notary at Kaskaskia. The notary handed over the documents to the British when the French government ceded Illinois to England. During the British and early years of American rule, the old French notarial system essentially continued, although standards declined to some degree in the new and difficult circumstances. When the British abandoned Fort de Chartres in 1771, they moved the documents to Kaskaskia, where they remained until 1848, when they were transferred to the new county seat, Chester. Over the years, some records were lost, and the condition of the surviving documents deteriorated. But a wealth of information survives (fig. 2.3), now made available by the labors of Lawrie Cena Dean and Margaret Kimball Brown.[15]

By the early 1740s, increasing tensions between Britain and France led again to war, generally known in America as King George's War (1744–1748). The Illinois French militias were not called into service. The food production of Illinois was of greater importance than any military contribution of the local militias, particularly since British dominance on the seas severely restricted other sources of supplies to Louisiana. During the war, Illinois was almost isolated. New Orleans received few supplies from France and had little to send to Illinois. For a year and a half, the French in Illinois went without supplies of European goods.

Even after the official end of hostilities in 1748, British traders from the Eastern Seaboard colonies continued to penetrate beyond the Alleghenies into territory claimed by France and attempted to convince tribes

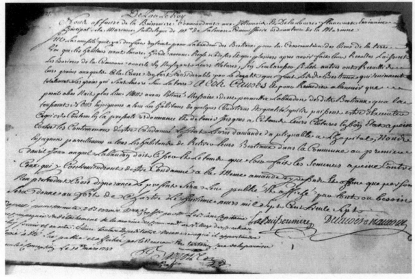

Fig. 2.3. Document of March 8, 1737, from the Kaskaskia Manuscripts: a public order of Commandant Alfonse de la Buissoniere and De la Loiere Flaucourt that livestock not be allowed to roam freely until after All Saints'; that all settlers maintain their part of the commons fence on pain of a hundred-livre fine payable to the hospital; and that livestock be enclosed on April 1. Following the order is a note by clerk Barrois notarizing that he registered the above for Captain Le Blanc, commandant at Kaskaskia, on March 10, 1737. Photo by M. K. Brown.

to abandon their relations with the French and ally with the English. Although the French were able to rebuff most of these attempts, it was a time of uncertainty, a virtual cold war between Britain and France in America, with the Native Americans exploited as surrogates.

In late 1751, a new commandant, Jean-Jacques de Macarty Mactique, of Irish descent, came to Illinois. One of his first acts was to conduct a new census. This was the most comprehensive census in the history of French Illinois, although far from perfect. The census lists the population in fourteen different categories according to age and status, types and numbers of farm animals, land under cultivation, and even the number of guns, amount of gunpowder, and lead at hand. Macarty's census listed in Kaskaskia 350 French, 246 black slaves, and 75 Indian slaves, totaling 571. This census, like the earlier censuses, simply missed some people and did not include the garrison and transients. Even if we allow as many as two hundred uncounted people in these categories, it is still apparent that, on the eve of the French and Indian War, Kaskaskia, the largest of the French villages in Illinois, was still a small place.[16]

Macarty also had Fort de Chartres rebuilt in stone on a much-enlarged scale to house a greatly increased garrison of nearly three hundred marines (fig. 2.4). About the same time, farmers also established a new community on the western side of the Mississippi, a few miles north of Kaskaskia, called Ste. Geneviève, which today is the site of the greatest number of preserved French colonial structures in America, many similar to those that once stood in Kaskaskia.

Throughout the first years of the 1750s, relations between the British and French deteriorated, and violent incidents multiplied. The official declaration of war in 1756 was almost anticlimactic. During the French and Indian War, 1756–1763, no combat took place in French Illinois, but men from Kaskaskia and the other French villages played an important but often ignored role in the war. They, along with soldiers and allied Indians, repeatedly rowed and portaged almost 1,400 arduous miles to supply flour and salted meat to the garrisons of the French forts that clustered around the watershed of the Ohio River (fig. 2.5). Men from Illinois also fought British forces, winning several creditable victories and suffering a costly loss at the Battle of La Belle Famille close to Fort Niagara in 1759.

The end of the French and Indian War disrupted long-standing relationships of French, English, and Indians throughout the Midwest. Tribes such as the Kickapoo, Shawnee, and Cherokee raided and, in some

Fig. 2.4. Fort de Chartres, reconstructed on original foundations. Photograph courtesy of Joseph Gagné.

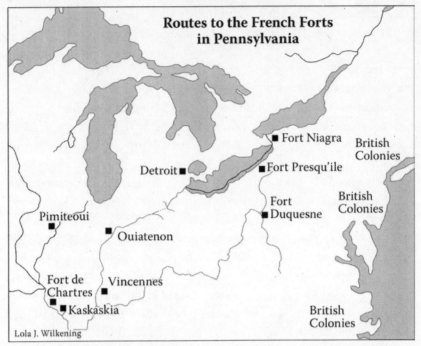

Fig. 2.5. Wabash and Ohio River routes from Illinois to the French forts.

cases, migrated into Illinois. About 1760, Prisque Pagé (also Paget) of Kaskaskia built a mill on the east side of the Kaskaskia River, a little to the north of the town.[17] Previously the people of Kaskaskia had relied on horse-powered mills and windmills. Philip Pittman, a British officer who visited Illinois in 1788, wrote,

> Another great advantage that Cascasquias receives from its river is the facility with which mills for corn and planks may be erected on it. Mons. Paget was the first who introduced water-mills in this country, and he constructed a very fine one on the river Cascasquias, which was both for grinding corn and sawing boards; it lies about a mile from the village. The mill proved fatal to him, being killed as he was working in it, with two negroes, by a party of Cherokees, in the year 1764.[18]

The Indians beheaded Pagé and threw his head into the grain hopper. After his death the mill was abandoned, but it was eventually rebuilt several times and served Kaskaskia and the region into the twentieth century.

CHAPTER 3

KASKASKIA AND INDIAN KASKASKIA UNDER BRITISH AND EARLY AMERICAN RULE, 1765–1790

KASKASKIA IN THE BRITISH PERIOD, 1765–1778

THE COLLAPSE OF French defenses in North America in 1760 and France's defeats in Europe and elsewhere led to the 1763 Treaty of Paris ending the Seven Years' War, but the treaty brought no peace to North America. Chief Pontiac inspired a loose coalition of tribes, not ready to accept British sovereignty, to capture or besiege British forts across a wide swath of North America. Although Pontiac's efforts ultimately failed, the hostilities delayed the British occupation of Illinois until 1765, when a detachment of the British Forty-Second Regiment of Foot journeyed down the Ohio and then up the Mississippi, where the soldiers stopped briefly at Kaskaskia and then proceeded to Fort de Chartres. In accordance with provisions of the treaty that had ended the war, the last French commandant of the fort, Louis St. Ange de Bellerive, turned over the fort to the British, ending the French regime in Illinois.

St. Ange, along with about forty troops and a few French administrators, moved to the new settlement of St. Louis on the western bank of the Mississippi, which the French monarchy had ceded to Spain at the end of the Seven Years' War. St. Ange commanded there until 1770, when a Spanish governor finally arrived.[1] During the following years, Spanish bureaucrats generally occupied the highest offices, but French men (often Creoles) continued to be prominent at many levels. There were a few Spanish troops at Ste. Geneviève and a small garrison at St. Louis. Local militias met more or less regularly but served only rarely. Despite the military weakness of the Spanish, the British across the Mississippi viewed the Spanish and the French serving in the Spanish administration with suspicion and trepidation.

The British occupied the eastern side of the Mississippi, but they can hardly be said to have governed. Between 1765 and 1776, seven British officers served as commandants of Illinois. None remained long, and there was little consistency in administration. None had adequate resources, all lacked competency in civil administration, some had unsuitable temperaments, and several were grossly corrupt. Dishonest land speculators and British merchant companies contributed to the maladministration. The local French population and a few English traders and merchants repeatedly petitioned to replace the arbitrary regime of military commandants with civil government according to English law. The British administration, largely concerned with growing problems in the Eastern Seaboard colonies, initially ignored the petitions.[2]

In 1765, Captain Philip Pittman of the British army accompanied Major Robert Farmar's convoy from New Orleans to Fort de Chartres and the Illinois Country. In 1770, he published his account of the voyage and the settlements along the Mississippi:

> The village of Notre Dame de Cascasquias is by far the most considerable settlement in the country of the Illinois, as well from its number of inhabitants as from its advantageous situation; its stands on the side of a small river, which is about eighty yards across; its source lies north-east, about sixty leagues from the village, and fifteen leagues east of the remarkable rock of Peorya*,[3] and it empties itself with a gentle current into the Mississippi, near two leagues below the village. The river is a secure port for large bateaux, which can lie so close to its bank as to load and unload without the least trouble; and at all seasons of the year there is water enough for them to come up. It must be observed here, that it is extremely dangerous for bateaux or boats to remain in the Mississipi, on account of the bank falling in, and the vast number of logs and trees which are sent down with a violent force, by the rapidity of the current, as also on account of the heavy gales of wind to which this climate is subject. . . . The principal buildings are, the church and Jesuits house, which has a

small chapel adjoining to it; these, as well as some other houses in the village, are built of stone, and, considering this part of the world, make a very good appearance. The Jesuits plantation consisted of two hundred and forty *arpens* of cultivated land, a very good stock of cattle, and a brewery; which was sold by the French commandant, after the country was ceded to the English, for the crown, in consequence of the suppression of the order. Mons. Beauvais was the purchaser, who is the richest of the English subjects in this country; he keeps eighty slaves; he furnished eighty-six thousand weight of flour to the king's magazine, which was only a part of the harvest he reaped in one year. Sixty-five families reside in this village, besides merchants, other casual people, and slaves. The fort, which was burnt down in October, 1766, stood on the summit of a high rock opposite the village, and on the other side of the river; it was an oblongular quadrangle, of which the exterior polygon measured two hundred and ninety by two hundred and fifty-one feet; it was built of very thick squared timber, and dove-tailed at the angles. An officer and twenty soldiers are quartered in the village. The officer governs the inhabitants, under the direction of the commandant at fort Chartres. Here are also two companies of militia.

  * There is in a sort of nich in this rock a figure that bears some resemblance to a man; the Indians who pass by pay their adorations to it, imagining it something supernatural, and that it has influence over their fortunes.[4]

Pittman, a qualified surveyor, also provided the first plan of Kaskaskia. On the plan of the village (figs. 3.1, 3.2), Pittman indicates the location of the former Jesuit compound that became Fort Gage (B), the commandant's residence (C), and the church (D). The irregular enclosures on the plan represent palisade enclosures of standing posts planted side by side in the earth.[5] Such palisades, in the Illinois Country preferably made of rot-resistant mulberry or cedar and standing five to six feet high, generally surrounded building complexes, such as the church and parochial residence, stores and storage sheds, or, most commonly, a single residence and outbuildings (such as a barn, chicken coop, and dovecote) and garden. As depicted on Pittman's plan, however, many of these enclosures are much larger and contain more buildings than would be expected of any single establishment. Moreover, the buildings

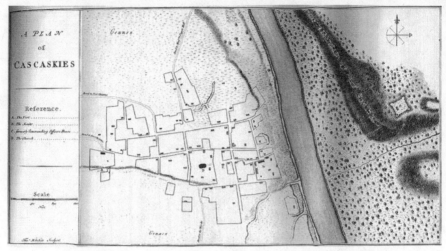

Fig. 3.1. *A Plan of Cascaskies*, a map made from Captain Philip Pittman's measurements and the plate engraved by Thomas Hutchins. From Pittman, *The Present State of the European Settlements on the Mississippi* (London: printed for J. Nourse, 1770), between pp. 8 and 9.

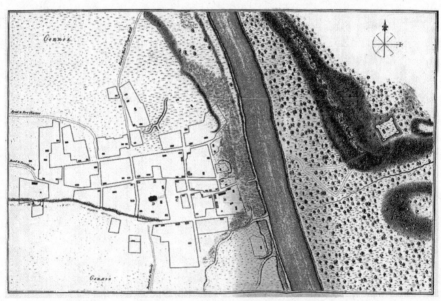

Fig. 3.2. *A Plan of Cascaskies*, magnified and cropped to show detail. Pittman, *Present State*.

are scattered rather than grouped logically for single establishments. Pittman apparently mapped the joined exterior palisades of properties but not the interior palisade walls subdividing some of the properties, to which he probably had no access. The buildings he indicates were major structures, such as residences, and he apparently ignored minor structures, such as dovecotes and stables. The irregular pattern of streets and enclosures testifies to the random growth of early Kaskaskia, in contrast to the geometrically regular grids of the planned French towns of southern Louisiana laid out by government surveyors.

In 1766, the Philadelphia trading company of Bayton, Wharton, and Morgan sent John Jennings to supervise the shipment of goods to Fort de Chartres. Jennings kept a journal, including observations about French Kaskaskia and a rare comment about Indian Kaskaskia. Jennings's contempt for Kaskaskia and its French inhabitants, who he thought presented "a very droll appearance," is typical of the sort of attitude that alienated the French:

Saturday 5th April.

At Six O'Clock this Morning left our Camp, at Eight heard a gun fire, & saw the St George's Colours hoisted, which gave us great pleasure, immediately answered it, & hoisted the Union flag. at Ten O'Clock came up to them at the Mouth of the Kuskuskes River. . . . at Two O'Clock in the afternoon arrived at the Village, which is situated by the River side, on a very extensive plain, with some very rich soil about it. It hath a Number of houses, some Large, but meanly built, with good Lotts behind them for Gardens, but make little use of them. the inhabitants in general being very indolent yet some are wealthy. at this time most of the principal of them, are gone on the Spanish side the Mississippi, with their Cattle & Corn, which makes provisions very Scarce, the Streets are Irregular, has a tolerable Good Church, & a Large Colledge, but is abandon'd, all the preists being gone away.

Sunday 6th.

At two O'Clock this afternoon, left the Kuskuskes, to proceed for Fort Chartres . . . on the Road leading to this place, about four Miles from the Kuskuskes is an Indian Town, the Nation of the above Name. Their Head Cheif Tomera, It hath several Houses & a Large Church in it.[6]

After the arrival of the British, many French moved from Kaskaskia and the other villages on the British east side of the Mississippi across to the Spanish side. Some relocated immediately; more followed over the course of time, discouraged by the contemptuous, inept, and oppressive character of British rule and attracted by economic opportunities in what is now Missouri. Other French remained on the eastern side of the river, long preserving their French linguistic and cultural character. Some moved back and forth across the Mississippi as economic and personal interests changed. Those who left Kaskaskia migrated mainly to Ste. Geneviève, New Madrid, and other new settlements south of Ste. Geneviève.

Despite the emigration of a significant portion of the population to the Spanish side of the Mississippi, the population of Kaskaskia retained sufficient vitality to undertake a major construction project in 1775. The old stone church, built 1737–1740, had become dangerously unstable. The moist, soft soil of Kaskaskia did not offer a firm basis for heavy buildings, and as the foundations of the church had shifted and settled, dangerous fissures appeared in the walls. In 1775, the congregation abandoned the stone church and erected a new church of vertical logs.[7] The new church was probably built with the *poteaux sur sol* technique, with vertical timbers mortised into timber sills and head plates, and the areas between the vertical timbers filled with material such as clay and grass or stones in clay. It was an impressive structure, apparently much like the surviving vertical-log church at Cahokia but larger and with a high steeple.

In 1771, the British abandoned Fort de Chartres. The Mississippi had changed course, eroding the riverbank and encroaching on the fort. The fort's riverside wall collapsed in 1772. The British moved their garrison to Kaskaskia, where they occupied the old stone house that the Jesuits had abandoned in 1763. They surrounded it with a picket fence and built two wooden bastions in which they placed two small cannons and a few swivel guns brought from Fort de Chartres. They called this comically inadequate post Fort Gage. In 1772, the British withdrew most of their troops from Illinois. During the same year, the British finally began to discuss the formation of a civil government for Illinois, but the idea was abandoned as the Eastern Seaboard colonies moved toward rebellion.

In 1776, Captain Hugh Lord departed along with the last British troops in Illinois, called to the growing rebellion in the east. Lord left behind

Philippe-François de Rastel de Rocheblave as the sole representative of the British government in Illinois, a complex man with a complex history. He was born into an aristocratic military family, rose to the rank of captain in the French marines, and served bravely in combat. Rocheblave was the city commandant of Kaskaskia during the last years of the French regime, and after the British arrived, he crossed over to the Spanish side of the river, where he served as the commandant of Ste. Geneviève. When Spanish officials in New Orleans displayed less than full confidence in Rocheblave, he felt insulted and left to return to the British side of the river. There he befriended Captain Lord, who recommended his appointment.

The British intended for Rocheblave to be a simple functionary, to do no more than publicize British decrees, preside over the court at Kaskaskia, and write reports on any suspicious Spanish or Indian activities. Rocheblave, however, intended to act fully as the commandant of the Illinois Country. He dealt ably with a wide variety of issues, attempted to balance French and English interests, displeasing both, and far exceeded his allotted budget. When the Revolutionary War broke out, Rocheblave repeatedly warned the British that Illinois was vulnerable to attack by the American rebels. He had no British troops, and although he could attempt to call out the local militias, it was highly unlikely they would respond. The militias had repeatedly refused to serve under previous British commandants. Had the British listened to Rocheblave and sent even a small defensive force of British regulars to Kaskaskia, American history might have been much different.[8]

KASKASKIA DURING THE EARLY
AMERICAN PERIOD, 1778–1790

IN 1778, THE American Revolution came to Kaskaskia. Early in the war, George Rogers Clark proved himself an able militia leader in Kentucky. In 1778, Patrick Henry, governor of Virginia, authorized Clark to lead an expedition to take the Illinois Country, hoping to curtail raids into Kentucky by British-allied Indians. Virginia at this time claimed territory far to the west of its current borders, even as far as the Mississippi River. Clark moved down the Ohio River with only 175 men into the vicinity of the abandoned French Fort Massiac, today Metropolis, Illinois, virtually across the river from modern Paducah, Kentucky. There he began

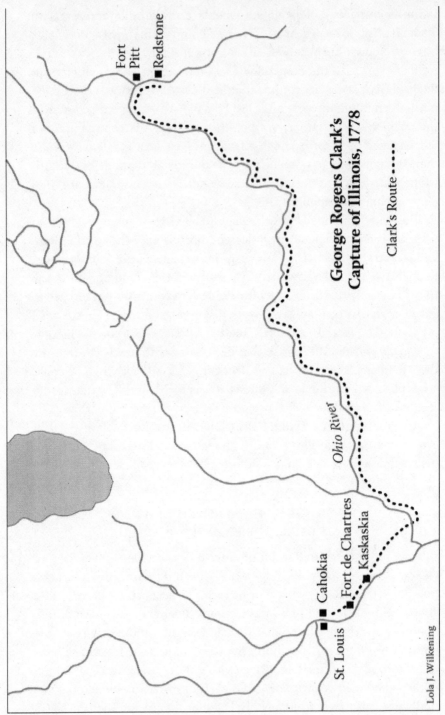

Fort Pitt

Redstone

**George Rogers Clark's
Capture of Illinois, 1778**

Clark's Route ▪▪▪▪▪

Ohio River

Cahokia

Fort de Chartres

Kaskaskia

St. Louis

Lola J. Wilkening

Fig. 3.3. Clark's campaign in Illinois.

a cross-country trek of about 120 miles to Kaskaskia, which Clark and his men occupied without resistance (fig. 3.3). Rocheblave and his wife were taken prisoner in their quarters.

Clark wrote two dramatic accounts of his first few days in Kaskaskia that emphasized his masterly command of the situation and the terrified reaction of the inhabitants. According to Clark, for several days after taking Kaskaskia, he played upon the fears of the inhabitants of the village, until they broke down: "Giving all for lost their Lives were all they could dare beg for, which they did with greatest fervancy; they were willing to be Slaves to save their Families."[9] At this point, Clark broke the tension by proclaiming that the Americans guaranteed the inhabitants' religious freedom and property rights, and he revealed the alliance of the Americans with France against Britain. Led by Father Pierre Gibault, the Kaskaskians enthusiastically declared their loyalty to the American

Fig. 3.4. George Rogers Clark in old age, circa 1810. Painting attributed to C. D. Cook. The only portraits of the young Clark are late, imaginative works. National Portrait Gallery, Smithsonian Institution.

cause and even accompanied Clark's forces as they peacefully occupied the other French settlements in the Illinois Country. These accounts should not be taken at face value.[10] Clark is ever the focus of his own narratives (fig. 3.4). He little appreciates others' motivations and exhibits a strong tendency to exaggerate the dramatic.

The people of Kaskaskia were certainly alarmed by the sudden appearance in their midst of 175 dirty, rude "long knives," as the Virginians were known, and Clark's proclamations did not turn alarm to instant enthusiasm for American rule. The British had guaranteed freedom of religion and property rights without winning the affection of the Illinois French. The French surely welcomed Clark's promises and news of the French alliance, but primarily their reason to cooperate was simple pragmatism.

The Illinois French had accepted British rule in 1765 because they could do nothing to resist it. In 1778, they had no real affection for the British and no motivation to resist American rule, which perhaps would be an improvement. Father Gibault, the so-called patriot priest, simply acted in the best interest of his people when he urged the people of Kaskaskia to accept Clark's occupation peacefully. Gibault and leading citizens of Kaskaskia similarly exhorted the other French villages of the American Bottom to submit to Clark. Then Gibault and Dr. Jean-Baptiste Laffont traveled to Vincennes, where they also gained the peaceful acceptance of American rule. The Illinois Indians were not slow to follow the lead of the French. Jean-Baptiste Ducoigne, the paramount chief of the Kaskaskia and most important chief among all the Illinois, provided Clark's forces with hunters and scouts and even negotiated with other tribes on Clark's behalf.[11]

The pragmatic character of French submission to American rule is most clearly evident in subsequent events at Vincennes. The men of that post duly signed the oath of allegiance that Father Gibault brought from Clark, renouncing loyalty to George III and swearing to be faithful and true subjects of "la République de la Virginie."[12] When Henry Hamilton, the British commandant at Detroit, recaptured Vincennes in December 1778, the inhabitants agreeably renounced their recent oath to Virginia and again swore allegiance to George III (fig. 3.5).

When Clark retook Vincennes after an epic march in terrible conditions, undoubtedly his greatest military achievement, the people of Vincennes promptly renounced their oath to the British king and again

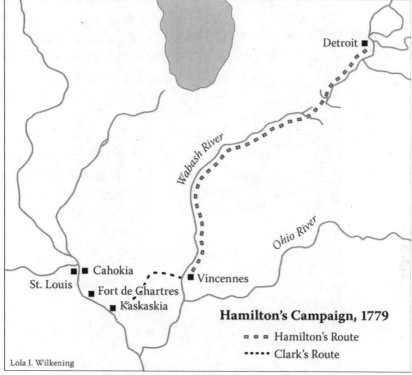

Fig. 3.5. Henry Hamilton's campaign to retake Illinois, 1779.

swore loyalty to Virginia, this time with some enthusiasm. Hamilton did not bother to hide his disdain for Vincennes and its inhabitants (fig. 3.6), and they in turn detested him.

While the retaking of Vincennes ended any immediate threat to Clark's hold on Illinois, Clark could not rest on his laurels. Many of his troops departed when their term of enlistment had expired, leaving him with barely one hundred men. He was able to raise two companies among the young Illinois French, one from Kaskaskia, but he never had as many men as he wished.

In 1779, Spain joined France in alliance with the American revolutionaries and declared war on Britain. The British dispatched a large force of Indians accompanied by a few French to attack Spanish St. Louis and Clark's forces at Cahokia. The small Spanish garrison, the French militias of St. Louis and Ste. Geneviève, and hastily assembled hunters and traders saved St. Louis, while Clark's forces turned back a smaller attack at Cahokia.

Fig. 3.6. Portrait of Henry Hamilton, white glass paste relief on clear glass
paste ground, signed on truncation of bust: "H. H. / T. F. 1786 (Henry
Hamilton / Tassie *fecit*)." Inscribed on the base in gold paint is the following:
"HENRY HAMILTON / LATE GOVERNOR OF THE ISLAND OF DOMINIQUE
IN THE / WEST INDIES. BORN 30TH NOV^r 1735. DIED 12TH SEPT^r 1796. //
WHILE MANLY COURAGE WITH THE GENTLEST MIND / WHILE EVERY
GRACE WITH EVERY VIRTUE JOIND / WHILE MODEST MERIT IS ALLOWED
DESERT / WITH SUCH SUPREME BENEVOLENCE OF HEART / WHILE TRUTH
CAN SUCH A PANEGYRIC GIVE / SO LONG OH HAMILTON THY NAME SHALL
LIVE." Harvard Art Museums, Bequest of Grenville L. Winthrop. https:// www.
harvardartmuseums.org/collections/object/229872?q=Henry+Hamilton.

That same year, Augustin Mottin de La Balme, a French cavalry officer who had served briefly in the American army, arrived in Illinois.
He raised a force of about eighty French and Indians, many from Kaskaskia, intending ultimately to take Detroit from the British. Soon after
the expedition began, a number of La Balme's men realized the scheme
was unrealistic and deserted. The rest captured and looted the British

trading post at St. Joseph (today Niles, Michigan), but the Miami, led by the young subchief Little Turtle, intercepted La Balme and killed him and most of his force in battle. The episode marks the rise to prominence of Little Turtle, who went on to be the greatest leader of the Miami and a dangerous foe of the US Army.

Clark remained actively engaged against the British and their Indian allies in Kentucky and Ohio until the end of the Revolution, but his career went into slow decline, ending in alcoholism and ruin. Similarly, the relations between the Illinois French and the Americans deteriorated after the first heady days of the American occupation of Kaskaskia.[13] Virginians who were quartered in French homes were rude, demanding, and bullying. French remonstrations met with threats and violence. American currency was nearly worthless. Few trusted promises to pay issued in the name of the distant government of Virginia, and in fact many were never paid. Clark established courts, but many of the judges proved dishonest. The government in Virginia sent John Todd to establish civilian government in Illinois, but the effort quickly collapsed into squabbling and bitter recriminations. Corrupt military and civilian officials formed alliances with equally corrupt land speculators. British-inspired Indians raided in the American Bottom, even to the outskirts of Kaskaskia itself.

In 1780, Clark withdrew his rangers from Illinois, except for a small garrison at Kaskaskia that remained until late in the next year. Clark established a new settlement, Fort Jefferson, a few miles south of the confluence of the Mississippi and Ohio Rivers, but the Chickasaw forced the abandonment of the settlement after little more than a year.[14] When Clark's rangers withdrew from Illinois, the French were glad to see them go, but there was far worse to come. Kaskaskia and the other villages of the American Bottom were left virtually without governance and protection, and the countryside was lawless. The people of Cahokia were generally able to maintain order, and the town even grew in population during this period, but in Kaskaskia conditions approached chaos.

The primary agent of disorder was John Dodge. Thomas Jefferson, governor of Virginia, sent Dodge to Illinois as Indian agent, but soon after the departure of Clark's troops, Dodge formed an unscrupulous alliance with merchants and land speculators. He raised a gang of thugs and seized the old Fort Kaskaskia (fig. 3.7). He rearmed the fort with two cannons from the British Fort Gage, trained the cannons on Kaskaskia, and thoroughly cowed the villagers.

Fig. 3.7. Earthworks of Fort Kaskaskia. Photograph
by MacDonald and Waters, spring 2015.

Dodge and his faction dominated, cheated, extorted, and abused
the people of Kaskaskia. Although Dodge and his faction were mostly
Americans and those victimized were chiefly French, this was not an
exclusively ethnic feud. Some French allied with Dodge, while a number of Americans sided with the French inhabitants of Kaskaskia. Both
sides sent multiple petitions to the government in Virginia, which did
nothing effective. Predatory British merchants, agents, and spies further
aggravated the situation. By 1787, Dodge moved to the Spanish side
of the Mississippi, but he continued to interfere in Illinois for several
more years.[15]

Ecclesiastical conflict also contributed to the disarray. In 1783, an
oversight by the pontifical bureaucracy led the bishops of both Québec
and Baltimore to claim ecclesiastical jurisdiction over the Illinois Country. The Bishop of Baltimore sent Father Pierre Huet de la Valinière to
Illinois as vicar-general, but the two priests already in Illinois, Fathers
Gibault and Paul de St. Pierre, served under the jurisdiction of Québec and did not recognize La Valinière's authority. All could have been
resolved by simply waiting for the church bureaucracy to decide the
matter, but La Valinière's personality permitted no such easy solution.
He was probably, by modern standards, mentally ill. Throughout his

career, he showed himself to be grandiose, quarrelsome, and aggressive. He attacked virtually everyone with whom he came into contact,
including Dodge, Fathers Gibault and De St. Pierre, and the inhabitants
of Cahokia and Kaskaskia. He so alienated the people of Kaskaskia that
they sent a petition to Congress condemning his furious disposition,
violent passions, unjust and indecent attacks from the pulpit, baseless
insults, threats, extortions, groundless excommunications, and theo-
cratic despotism, all backed with specific examples. Huet de la Valinière
finally left Illinois in 1789.[16]

To compound the distress even further, in 1785 the Mississippi flooded
to a height beyond memory. The American Bottom was inundated, and
Ste. Geneviève on the west bank and Kaskaskia on the east were badly
damaged. Every building in Kaskaskia was flooded. The year 1785 was
long remembered as *l'année des grandes eaux*, the year of big waters.
During three other years in this decade, natural disasters also ruined
the crops on which the Illinois villages depended.

During the decade of 1780–1790, the inhabitants of Kaskaskia experienced a general collapse of society. As Illinois slipped toward anarchy,
many Illinois French, including leading citizens of the town, crossed
to resettle on the Spanish side of the Mississippi.[17] Kaskaskia had 194
households when Clark arrived in 1778; by 1790 the town had declined to
44 households.[18] Before 1765, visitors described the inhabitants of Illinois
as prosperous and living well, but after 1790, American settlers often
depicted the Illinois French as poor and dispirited. A great historian
of the Mississippi Valley, John Francis McDermott, long ago pointed
out that their poverty was "not the result of a sinful indolence but of a
combination of circumstances imposed upon them and for which they
were helped to no remedy." It is likely that the idea that Kaskaskia suffered under a curse first arose in this period of calamities. Years later a
lament of Father Pierre Gibault, who ministered in Illinois throughout
this period, was taken as prophecy of the woeful fate of Kaskaskia.[19]

INDIAN KASKASKIA

JUST AS THE French at Kaskaskia suffered greatly through the period of
British and early American rule, so too did the Kaskaskia Indian tribe suf-
fer (fig. 3.8). By the second half of the eighteenth century, the population
of the Kaskaskia and the other Illinois tribes had declined precipitously

owing to European diseases, alcohol, and intertribal warfare. Contemporary estimates vary wildly, but it is apparent that the Illinois then numbered in the hundreds rather than the thousands.[20] Illinois tribes still claimed a large portion of Illinois as their territory, but they were badly outnumbered by other tribes that were encroaching on their territory. Old tribal feuds continued to provoke violence, and the Illinois were seldom able to defend themselves or their territory effectively.

Fig. 3.8. Member of the Kaskaskia tribe. Vignette from map. G. Bois St. Lys and J. J. Boudier, *Carte générale du cours de la rivière de l'Ohio . . . le tout dessiné sur les lieux par Joseph Warrin . . . pour servir à l'intelligence des voyages du général Collot dans l'année 1796*. Bibliothèque nationale de France, département des Cartes et plans, CPL GE A 664.

During the French and Indian War, 1756–1763, the British-allied Cherokee and Chickasaw attacked the Illinois. After 1765, the British were able to arrange a peace between these tribes, but tensions remained high; in 1772, violence broke out at Kaskaskia again when both the Kaskaskia and Chickasaw came to trade.[21] British troops intervened to restore order in this local disturbance, but they were unable to protect the Kaskaskia from their old enemies, the Fox and Sauk. From at least the late seventeenth century, the Fox and Illinois had been inveterate enemies. In 1730, the Illinois were part of an alliance of tribes that, along with the French, almost wiped out the Fox. By midcentury, however, the Fox had revived. They, along with the Sauk and other allies, raided the Cahokia and Michigamea in 1752, killing about eighty,[22] and more raids followed in the next decades.

During the difficult last quarter of the eighteenth and first decade of the nineteenth century, Jean-Baptiste Ducoigne was the paramount chief of the Kaskaskia and often the leader and spokesman of all the Illinois. An able leader, Ducoigne dominated the history of Indian Kaskaskia, of the Kaskaskia tribe, and of all the Illinois Indians in this period, but the Kaskaskia and Illinois as a whole had so declined in numbers that Ducoigne was never able to function from a position of strength.

The name Ducoigne is spelled variously as De Couagne, Decouagne, Decougner, Decoigne, Dequoney, Dequones, Du Coigne, Du Coign, Ducoin, Ducoine, Du Quoin, Ducain, Docouogne, Deguen, and perhaps a few other ways. Jean-Baptiste de Couagne, who became the father of the Kaskaskian chief Jean-Baptiste Ducoigne, was born in Montréal to a mercantile family.[23] He first traveled to the Illinois Country about 1736 as an *engagé*, an employee under contract. Between 1742 and 1747, the Kaskaskia Manuscripts indicate that he was operating as a trader at Vincennes and Kaskaskia. At some point, he entered into a liaison or tribal marriage with Elisabeth-Michel Rouensa, a member of the leading family among the Kaskaskia. The oft-repeated assertion that Jean-Baptiste Ducoigne was born to this couple in 1750 and baptized at Ste. Anne's by Fort de Chartres is wrong.

The parish record indicates that on January 22, 1750, the priest baptized a child of the Indian woman Elisabeth-Michel Rouensa and "Le pere est un nomme de couagne" (the father is a man of the name de couagne), but the child was named Louis, not Jean-Baptiste.[24] No baptismal record survives for Jean-Baptiste, so despite the difference in name, it has often been assumed that the child was Jean-Baptiste. It is much more likely that Louis was Jean-Baptiste's brother. This Louis appears in no other document and probably died young, as did so many other children in the eighteenth century. It is not surprising that no baptismal record survives for Jean-Baptiste. His father spent more time at Vincennes than Kaskaskia, and the only baptismal records surviving from Vincennes are from much later.

R. M. Owens suggests, "Baptised as Louis, the future chief apparently changed his name probably at his pubertal vision quest, as was common among the Illinois tribes."[25] Owens's argument is weak, leading back to only a single source on vision quests among the Illinois Indians, written almost a century before Ducoigne's adolescence, long before the culture of the Kaskaskia had been substantially altered by conversion to Christianity, and even that does not mention name changes. Ducoigne's father was French and his mother was from a family that had been Catholic since the late seventeenth century. No source indicates that Jean-Baptiste Ducoigne or any other of the long-Christianized Kaskaskia went on vision quests in the late eighteenth century. In the unlikely event that Jean-Baptiste did go on such a quest and decided to change his name, he would have changed his Indian name, not his Catholic baptismal name.[26]

The baptismal record of Louis Ducoigne is nevertheless important. It reveals that the mother of Louis and Jean-Baptiste Ducoigne was a member of the Rouensa family, whose leaders were the paramount chiefs of the Kaskaskia from at least the late seventeenth century through much of the eighteenth century. Jean-Baptiste Ducoigne, connected to the traditional leadership of the Kaskaskia through his birth mother, would in time also become the paramount chief of the Kaskaskia.[27]

Jean-Baptiste Ducoigne's birth date is unknown, and the evidence bearing on the question is contradictory. S. Faye cites a Spanish source from 1775 that describes Jean-Baptiste as "mozo como de 20 años" (a young man about twenty years old), which would imply a birth date of 1755, but Jean-Baptiste became a chief of the Kaskaskia in 1767.[28] The Kaskaskia, like most other tribes, had a number of chiefs, some with specific functions, and a paramount chief. It is inconceivable that even a scion of the Rouensa family became a chief at the age of twelve. At a minimum, a chief would be expected to be in his twenties, an age that corresponds with his father's activities in the Illinois Country. Our only physical description of Jean-Baptiste, made later in his life, describes him as a small, athletic man.[29] The Spanish official, who met Jean-Baptiste only once and then briefly, probably underestimated Jean-Baptiste's age or mistook Ducoigne's spokesman for the chief himself. Ducoigne did not speak Spanish, and the official did not speak Illinois. Jean-Baptiste was most likely born during the 1740s.

We know nothing of Jean-Baptiste's early life, but he undoubtedly owed early prominence to his connection to the Rouensa family, but that alone would not have sufficed to make him the leader of his people. Among the Illinois, the position of chief tended to be hereditary but not strictly or inevitably so. The warriors selected chiefs by acclamation, but heredity assured a man only of consideration. The warriors would reject a man who had failed to distinguish himself as a warrior, hunter, and orator, despite even the strongest claims of family connections, and turn to a more worthy candidate. Jean-Baptiste's later career indicates that, among his other talents, he was an able orator in the Indian tradition and, although illiterate, fluent in both Illinois and French, a significant talent even after a century of interaction between the two cultures.

In 1766, Jean-Baptiste was at Detroit along with two other Illinois, one a principal chief, when Pontiac stabbed the chief in a dispute about inter-tribal relations. At some time during the same year or early in 1767, a chief of the Kaskaskia, called Pedigogue by the English, died, and Jean-Baptiste succeeded to his position as a chief but not the paramount chief. The stabbed chief may have been Pedigogue, and the injury may have caused his death, but decisive evidence is lacking. The British Indian agent Edward Cole, in writing to the British superintendent of Indian affairs George Croghan, described Jean-Baptiste's elevation:

> The nation [the Illinois] assembled before me in order to have another chief—Young Dequoney being the next heir, he was Unanimously pitched on if agreeable to me. I could have no objections known him to be a fine young fellow not Debaouched with Liquors, and from the readiness he Shews to receive advice and Good behavior, make me think he will become one of the Greatest chiefs in this country.[30]

During the French and Indian War, the Illinois had naturally supported the French, and they remained antagonistic to the British after the end of the war. When it became apparent that the British were the new power in Illinois, Jean-Baptiste Ducoigne helped forge a reconciliation with the British.

Kaskaskia parish records indicate that in 1771 Father Gibault, curé at Kaskaskia, baptized Françoise, the daughter of Jean-Baptiste and his wife Marie-Joseph. In 1772, Gibault baptized a second daughter, Thérèse-Hélène, daughter of Jean-Baptiste and his wife Hélène.[31] Marie-Joseph must have died soon after the birth of her daughter; rapid remarriage was common.

In late 1773 or early 1774, Tomera (Tamarois), the old paramount chief of the Kaskaskia, died, and the Kaskaskia chose Jean-Baptiste Ducoigne to succeed him. Ducoigne led the Kaskaskia during the next four decades and faced great challenges, utmost among which were murderous attacks on the Illinois by other tribes.

Ducoigne attempted to ensure the safety of his people even to the extent of leaving Illinois. In the autumn of 1774, he led many of the Kaskaskia, eighty families, down the Mississippi; others remained behind at Indian Kaskaskia. In the spring of 1775, Ducoigne and his followers traveled up the Arkansas River to join the Quapaw at the Spanish Fort Carlos III. The Spanish commander Don Josef de Orieta offered them land to farm at the Quapaw village, but the Kaskaskia proposed to establish a separate village up the White River; the commandant refused permission. The sources contain no explicit reason for his refusal, but he may have feared a potential loss of trade through his post or felt a need to keep close watch on the Kaskaskia. Ducoigne traveled downriver to the Spanish post of Fort San Gabriel de Manchac, the most northerly Spanish post on the eastern bank of the Mississippi, and there he gave a petition to the Spanish commandant Don Thomas de Acosta to forward to governor Don Luis de Unzaga y Amézaga. The governor supported the commander at Arkansas and refused permission for the separate village.[32]

During their time in Arkansas, Jean-Baptiste Ducoigne and Hélène had another child, a son named Jean-Baptiste like his father. Two years later in Illinois, Father Gibault baptized Jean-Baptiste *fils*.[33]

The outbreak of the American Revolution brought changes to the Kaskaskia. Spain supported the rebels against Britain, at first clandestinely, and the Kaskaskia in Arkansas played a role, attacking British traders on the Mississippi. As a reward, the Spanish governor, now Don Bernardo de Gálvez, gave permission for Ducoigne and the Kaskaskia to settle on the White River, but instead, in late 1777, they ended their sojourn in Arkansas and headed north.[34]

Sources do not indicate Ducoigne's motivation, but he was aware of the quickly evolving situation and always sought to benefit the Kaskaskia. Spain and France both aided the American rebellion, and the Kaskaskia, like the Illinois French, had little affection for the negligent British, who failed to prevent hostile tribes from attacking the Kaskaskia who had remained in Illinois. In 1775, the Fox and Sauk came in war paint to Indian Kaskaskia. They found the village temporarily vacant and burned it. They also entered French Kaskaskia, where they searched for Kaskaskia Indians, but finding none, they left without molesting the French. They finally found the Kaskaskia across the Mississippi in their summer hunting camp on the River aux Vases. There, the Fox and Sauk killed forty-four Kaskaskia men, women, and children and took several prisoners at the cost of two of their chiefs and an unspecified number of warriors.[35] Some of the Kaskaskia returned to their burnt village, and others, including some Peoria, joined Ducoigne's band in a village on the Spanish side of the Mississippi roughly forty miles south of Ste. Geneviève.[36]

In a rapid campaign in early summer of 1778, George Rogers Clark and a small force seized Illinois. Clark wrote that the Kaskaskia and Peoria, led by Ducoigne, immediately sought peace and alliance, and Ducoigne provided Clark with hunters and scouts. Ducoigne did more; he negotiated for Clark with other tribes. Agents of Henry Hamilton, British commandant at Detroit, reported Ducoigne's activities with the Miami on Clark's behalf, and Ducoigne also attempted repeatedly to bring the Chickasaw into alliance with Clark.[37] Then, before the end of 1778, Ducoigne went east to Virginia, where he and about a hundred warriors fought under Lafayette against the British. Lafayette presented Ducoigne with a written appreciation of his service.[38]

Returning to Illinois, Ducoigne had to face bitter reality. Clark withdrew most of his forces from Illinois in 1780 and the remainder shortly thereafter. The Kaskaskia and other Illinois were left to their own inadequate resources. The Fox, Sauk, Potawatomi, Kickapoo, Shawnee, and even the Cherokee and Chickasaw all raided the Illinois and encroached on their territory. The Illinois struck back when they could, but seldom and usually with little success. Ducoigne, often speaking for the Peoria as well as the Kaskaskia and even for all the Illinois, could only cling to the hope that the alliance with the Americans would eventually provide protection, but for years there was little American presence and power in the new western territory.

In 1781, Jean-Baptiste Ducoigne journeyed to meet with Thomas Jefferson, then governor of Virginia, in a show of mutual alliance, but little came of it, as each party sought ends that were essentially unrelated. The Americans were concerned with the continuing British threat from their base at Detroit, while Ducoigne and the Kaskaskia sought American protection against tribes moving into their territory.[39] Nevertheless, Jean-Baptiste was impressed with Jefferson and named his second son Louis-Jefferson Ducoigne, probably born shortly after Jean-Baptiste met Jefferson.[40] Ducoigne could only hope that American ideals and policies would eventually benefit his people.

CHAPTER 4

MIXED FORTUNES, 1790–1820

POLITICAL DEVELOPMENTS

IN 1787, THE Congress of the Confederation of the United States passed the Northwest Ordinance. The states surrendered their western land claims, including the Illinois Country, to the federal government, which formed them into the Northwest Territory, with the ultimate intention of promoting settlement toward the establishment of new states. Until the requirements for statehood could be met, the ordinance provided that the territory be administered by a governor, secretary, three judges, and, when the population reached five thousand free males, an elected general assembly.

The Revolutionary War general Arthur St. Clair (fig. 4.1), who served as president of the United States in Congress Assembled when the Northwest Ordinance was enacted, became the first governor of the Northwest Territory, establishing his headquarters at Fort Washington (today Cincinnati).

Settlers, land companies, and the federal government coveted the land of the Indian tribes in the territory, and the tribes centered along the Wabash River bitterly opposed the intrusion of Americans into the area. In late 1790, General Joseph Harmar moved against the Miami at Kekionga (today Fort Wayne) with a force of 1,453, the great majority of whom were untrained and ill-disciplined militiamen. Under the leadership of Little Turtle, the Miami and their allies defeated Harmar's forces in several engagements, killing over 200.

In late 1791, St. Clair brought together about 2,000 men—regulars, six-month conscripts, and militiamen—to move against the tribes on the

Fig. 4.1. Portrait of Arthur St. Clair, circa 1795, watercolor on ivory
by Jean Pierre Henri Elouis. National Portrait Gallery, Smithsonian
Institution; gift of Mr. and Mrs. Arthur St. Clair Johnson. Conserved
with funds from the Smithsonian Women's Committee.

upper Wabash. Not much had improved since the previous expedition.
The expedition was inadequately equipped, the conscripts and militiamen were poorly disciplined, and over 200 camp followers were allowed
to tag along on the expedition. By the time St. Clair camped near the
headwaters of the Wabash, desertion and illness had reduced his force to
920 officers and men. Little Turtle again proved a skillful leader. Under
his direction a confederation of tribes attacked and routed the American
force, killing 632 officers and men and about 200 camp followers. The
American wounded numbered 264; only 24 men escaped unscathed. The
Indians casualties were only about 20 dead and 40 wounded.[1]

After St. Clair's defeat, Little Turtle advised the tribes to seek peace,
but other leaders, intoxicated by the victories, rejected his advice. St.
Clair was replaced in command by Anthony Wayne (fig. 4.2), a more

careful and able general. In 1794, Wayne defeated the Indian coalition at the Battle of Fallen Timbers. The war ended by treaty the next year, and while the tribes were able to hold their lands for some years, they were eventually deprived of them and driven west.

Despite damage to his reputation, St. Clair continued as governor. He visited Kaskaskia briefly in 1790 when he organized St. Clair County, which included Kaskaskia, and he traveled to Kaskaskia again in 1795 when he created Randolph County out of a portion of St. Clair County, with Kaskaskia as its county seat. In 1800, the Northwest Territory was divided in preparation for the admission of Ohio as a state, and St. Clair became the governor of the Ohio Territory.

St. Clair's administration saw both achievements and missed opportunities. He and his small staff faced the difficult, perhaps impossible, task of administering with few resources a vast territory that now consists of Ohio, Indiana, Illinois, Michigan, and portions of Wisconsin and

Fig. 4.2. Portrait of Anthony Wayne, 1796, pastel on paper by James Sharples Sr. Courtesy of Independence National Historical Park.

Minnesota. He could, for instance, promulgate laws and establish courts, but he lacked the means to enforce their decisions. In a practice that was common at the time, St. Clair packed the newly established courts and offices with his relatives, friends, and supporters, whom he failed to supervise closely. Some proved to be incompetent, lazy, or dishonest. The court at Kaskaskia met only occasionally and earned a reputation for corruption. St. Clair established a territorial legislature and then quarreled incessantly with it. He made little progress in resolving land claims and temporized with the problem of slavery. An early amendment to the Northwest Ordinance banned slavery in the territory, but St. Clair merely prohibited the introduction of more slaves and took no measures concerning slaves already in the territory. That resulted in decades of political conflict between pro- and antislavery forces in Illinois. St. Clair earned a reputation for stubbornness, arrogance, and partisanship. He was a strong Federalist, and his political activities led President Jefferson to remove him from office in 1802.[2] William Henry Harrison then became the governor of the newly created Indiana Territory, which included Illinois.

In 1809, the federal government created the Illinois Territory, which included Illinois and the area that became Wisconsin. Kaskaskia was the territorial capital, the residence of the governor and secretary, and the meeting place of the territorial legislature, all symbolic of Kaskaskia's general revival, but progress was temporarily checked in the disastrous year of 1811. The Great Comet of 1811, large, bright, and long-lasting, was widely believed to have foretold the disasters that subsequently engulfed Kaskaskia that year: a flood ravaged crops, a tornado leveled part of the town, and then, in late 1811 and early 1812, the fearsome New Madrid earthquakes damaged much of what was left. The poorly consolidated, moist soil of Kaskaskia magnified the effects of the earthquakes. New Indian troubles also spread alarm in the Midwest. Tecumseh's unsuccessful attempt to form a grand confederation of tribes was followed by British-incited Indian violence during the War of 1812, generally taking the form of raids on isolated farmsteads. Several attacks took place near Kaskaskia, but most of the violence occurred to the north, and, other than the Fort Dearborn massacre (modern Chicago), most violence was small in scale. Alarm, however, was universal, and militiamen from Kaskaskia marched north to help protect settlers.[3] Despite the events of 1811–1812, Kaskaskia rebuilt and grew, and settlers in increasing numbers came to Illinois, most initially arriving at Kaskaskia. The territorial legislature continued to meet there, and the first newspaper in Illinois was published in Kaskaskia in 1814 (fig. 4.3).[4]

A generous estimate of the population of Illinois in 1818 places the number as perhaps as many as 36,000, but Congress initially required a territory to have a population of 60,000 for admission as a state. That seemed a distant prospect to the inhabitants of Illinois. Ohio had, however, been admitted as a state with fewer than 40,000 inhabitants, and Congress agreed to accept a population of just 40,000 in the case of Illinois. Illinois officials were in charge of the census and used creative though illicit means to reach that number. They grossly overestimated the populations of remote settlements and counted transients as residents, sometimes repeatedly at every stop of their journey. They even counted the inhabitants of Prairie du Chien, well north of the Illinois border. The total claimed was 40,258. No one believe the count to be accurate, but it was accepted; and on December 3, 1818, Illinois became a state and Kaskaskia its capital.[5]

Kaskaskia remained the capital during 1819, but the First Illinois General Assembly petitioned Congress to grant land for a new state capital. The new site, Vandalia, was founded in 1819, specifically to fulfill the role. Many specious reasons were adduced for the change. Kaskaskia was subject to flooding. A new capital built afresh could accommodate the seat of government with greater efficiency and dignity than rented rooms at Kaskaskia. The center of population was shifting away from the Mississippi Valley toward the center of the state and could be more efficiently served from Vandalia. The most important reason, however, was that speculators, including members of the legislature, intended to

Fig. 4.3. Masthead of the earliest surviving issue of the first newspaper in Illinois: the *Illinois Herald*, December 13, 1814, published at Kaskaskia. F. W. Scott, *Newspapers and Periodicals of Illinois, 1814–1878*, revised and enlarged ed., *Collections of the Illinois State Historical Library*, vol. 6, Biographical series 1 (Springfield: Illinois State Historical Library, 1910), frontispiece.

sell land at Vandalia at substantial profit. This corrupt political plot did
not prosper. Vandalia did not develop into a major metropolis, and the
capital was moved again, to Springfield, in 1839.

LOCAL CONDITIONS

CONDITIONS IN ILLINOIS did improve in the decade after 1790 but only
slowly and unevenly. Throughout the period, the Kaskaskia and other
Illinois tribes remained peaceful, though unhappy about squatters who
illegally carved farms out of their traditional hunting grounds. Other
tribes, some impelled by the events to the north, also intruded into the
territory claimed by the Illinois and attacked both white settlers and
the Kaskaskia and other Illinois tribes. Hostile Indians seldom threatened settlements, but in the countryside, small-scale violence remained
frequent. Whites and Indians both committed atrocities, which were
seldom punished legally but often led to violent retribution, and settlers
frequently made no distinction between friendly and hostile Indians. In
addition, bandits and river pirates preyed on travelers.

Few of the French who left to settle on the Spanish side of the Mississippi returned to Kaskaskia, but a steady though modest stream of
new settlers migrated to the town. French Canadians moved into the
Illinois Country by the traditional river routes and portages from the
north. The majority of Americans who entered Illinois and Missouri
came first to Kaskaskia. Many came from the South, but there were also
significant numbers from the Mid-Atlantic States and even New England. Most traveled on the Ohio River. Some tarried and even remained
at Shawneetown or Edwardsville, but the greatest number continued on
to Kaskaskia, either traveling all the way by water or disembarking at the
site of old Fort Massiac (modern Metropolis, Illinois) and then moving
across country. Many made Kaskaskia their permanent home, while others resided there for a time before moving on to establish farms, despite
the dangers of the countryside, or settle in the new towns developing in
Illinois. In such towns, modest businesses grew up, doing little cash business but retailing manufactured goods brought to Illinois by the great
wholesale merchants of St. Louis and Kaskaskia in exchange for farm
products that could be sold, often to those same wholesale merchants.
Many of the men who figured prominently in Illinois during the first
decades of nineteenth century came to Kaskaskia during this period.

By 1800, Kaskaskia was a bilingual town and prosperous to a degree
that few could have foreseen a decade earlier. The town benefited from
growing commerce on the Mississippi, the influx of settlers to Illinois
and Missouri, and the Indian trade. The great profits of the Indian trade
went not to the daring mountain men who traveled far to the west to
trap and trade furs but rather to the merchants who provided them with
supplies and trade goods and bought their furs for resale. A generation
of entrepreneurs, virtual merchant princes, emerged at St. Louis and to a
lesser extent at Kaskaskia. William Morrison, Pierre Ménard, John Edgar,
and others grew rich at Kaskaskia, and their prosperity was reflected in
the growth of the town. Land speculation was another source of wealth.
Investors, often partnerships of leading figures in the community, purchased large parcels of land, which they subdivided and sold to small
farmers at a profit. Agriculture also brought money into the area. John
Edgar, Revolutionary War officer and later general of the Illinois militias,
rebuilt the old Pagé mill about 1795 to take advantage of increased grain
production in the region. Flour was always in demand in New Orleans.

John Reynolds, the fourth governor of Illinois, published his auto-
biography in 1855, including an account of his first vision of Kaskaskia
as a boy in 1800. Although published long after the event, the account
retains a fresh vivacity and convincing attention to those factors that
would most attract the attention of a boy:

> When we approached the high Bluffs east of Kaskaskia we halted our
> traveling caravan, and surveyed with wonder and delight the prospect
> before us. It was in the spring, and the scenery was beautiful.
>
> The eye ranged up and down the American Bottom for many miles,
> and the whole landscape lay, as it were at our feet. The river bluffs
> rose two hundred feet or more above the bottom, and the prairie lay
> extended before our view, covered with cattle and horses grazing on
> it. The Mississippi itself could be seen in places through the forest
> of cotton-wood trees skirting its shores, and the ancient village of
> Kaskaskia presented its singular form and antique construction to
> our sight. The ancient Cathedral stood a venerable edefice [sic] in
> the heart of the village, with its lofty steeple, and large bell—the first
> church bell I ever saw. Around the village were numerous camps, and
> lodges of the Kaskaskia Indians, still retaining much of the original
> savage independence.

The large common field with a fence stretched out from the Kaskaskia river to the Mississippi extended on one side of the village, and the commons covered with cattle on the other. Near the bluff on the East, the Kaskaskia river wended its way South, and entered the Mississippi six miles below the village of Kaskaskia. . . .

The Kaskaskia Indians were numerous, and had still retained some of their savage customs. Many of the young warriors decorated themselves in their gaudy and fantastic attire with paints. Feathers of birds were tied in their hair; and sometimes the horns of animals were also attached to their heads. They galloped in this fantastic dress around our encampment.

This was a kind of salutation more to demonstrate their persons and their exploits than any thing else.

After recruiting a short time, and obtaining some provisions for ourselves, and food for our horses from the grist mill of General Edgar, which was "hard by," my father had his humble caravan prepared to cross the Mississippi and "all aboard," when some gentlemen from Kaskaskia came to our encampment and held a conversation with my father. These gentlemen were Messrs. Robert Morrison, John Rice Jones, Pierre Menard, and John Edgar, who debated the subject with my father, whether it was not better for him to remain at Kaskaskia sometime, and look around for a permanent residence. The argument of these gentlemen prevailed, and my parents agreed to take a house in Kaskaskia, and examine the country "around about."[6]

On November 29, 1803, Meriwether Lewis and William Clark arrived at Kaskaskia, where they consulted with leading citizens Pierre Ménard, John Edgar, and William Morrison. They also recruited twenty-five men to take part in their great expedition to the Pacific, some from the two army companies stationed at Fort Kaskaskia, others from men of French heritage. The men from Kaskaskia were the largest group recruited by Lewis and Clark and included men with skills that would prove vital to the expedition. Clark and the men of the Corps of Discovery left Kaskaskia on December 3, 1803. Lewis remained behind for a few days to deal with bureaucratic matters.

During the period from 1800 to 1820, Kaskaskia experienced mixed fortunes. Kaskaskia was politically important, economically prosperous, and the home of Illinois's leading citizens, but the town also suffered from great natural disasters; and in 1820, a corrupt political deal moved the capital of Illinois from Kaskaskia to Vandalia, a blow more significant than all the natural catastrophes. The shift of the capital and the center of political power away from Kaskaskia marginalized the French. After the end of the Revolutionary War, English-speaking Americans moved to Illinois in ever-increasing numbers and came to outnumber the French speakers, but as long as Kaskaskia remained the focus of settlement and political power, French language and culture remained of central importance alongside the growing American influences. The use of English grew increasingly common, particularly in business, but for many, French remained the language of family life and social interaction. In the decades after 1820, however, Kaskaskia's population declined as people relocated to Vandalia, to new towns developing in Illinois, and to St. Louis. French language and culture survived in the old French settlements, but English-speaking Americans increasingly came to regard Kaskaskia as a quaint, antiquated relic and the French as somehow.foreign and alien. The recurrent disasters and decline of the town after losing its status as the capital likely contributed to the belief that a curse lay over it, although the notion seems to have remained nebulous and unconnected to any particular event.

INSTITUTIONS

House of the Territorial and State Legislature

By far the most photographed structure in Kaskaskia was the building used as the meeting place for the Illinois territorial legislature from 1809 to 1818 and the state legislature from 1818 to 1820 (figs. 4.4, 4.5). Writers give several dates for the construction of the building, generally without any indication of their sources. Gustave Pape's account is most likely correct: "In the fall of 1866 I went into business for myself, having bought the brick building in which the old Territorial Legislature used to meet, and where the first State Constitutional Convention met in 1818. The brick of this building were brought from Pittsburg[h] in 1803."[7]

The basic shape of the building is Federal style, but the configuration of doors, windows, and chimneys is anything but traditional Federal. The main entrance, which served the first floor, was in the center of the gable end of the building. The door at the left end of the "front" of the building led to the second floor. The building may have been designed originally as a combination of residence and business.

Fig. 4.4. Territorial and State House with the Church of the Conception in the background. Bateman and Selby, eds., *Historical Encyclopedia of Illinois* (Chicago: Munsell, 1918), following p. 314.

Fig. 4.5. Territorial and State House. John Corson Smith, *History of Freemasonry in Illinois* (Chicago: Rogers and Smith, 1905), between pp. 44 and 45.

Note the two S-shaped forms on the gable, the larger one centered above the door and the small one still higher on the double chimney. This is a typical form for an iron end piece attached to an iron beam that ran through the wall, for the entire length of a building and through the opposite wall, where it was attached to a similar end piece and often incorporated a mechanical arrangement by which the beam could be shortened to pull together and strengthen brick walls damaged by earthquakes, such as struck Kaskaskia in 1811 and 1812.[8] The walls of the building were covered with a layer of lime mortar. An addition to the building covered by clapboards was entered by a separate door. The shed attached to the clapboard addition may have been a stable.

The building was put to many uses over the years. In 1806, the first Masonic Lodge in Illinois met on the second floor. From 1809 until 1818, the territorial legislature met in the same room, and Elias Kent Kane drafted the state's first constitution there. From 1818 to 1820, the state legislature met in the same room. Eventually, Gustave Pape opened his grocery there. The building collapsed into the Mississippi in 1900.

The Kaskaskia Court House

The erection of the Kaskaskia Court House was symbolic of the new prosperity of Kaskaskia in the second decade of the nineteenth century (fig. 4.6). In 1790, Arthur St. Clair established the large county of St. Clair, grandiosely named after himself. St. Clair divided the county into three judicial districts, Cahokia, Prairie du Rocher, and Kaskaskia.[9] In 1795, St. Clair separated Randolph County out of St. Clair County and designated Kaskaskia as the county seat. From 1790 until 1818, the court at Kaskaskia met wherever space allowed, in a residence, store, or tavern, but in 1819, at the height of Kaskaskia's prosperity, the town decided to build a courthouse. The *Illinois Intelligencer* for September 29, 1819, carried an announcement: "The County Commissioners of Randolph County will take bids on the building of a brick Court House in Kaskaskia until October 28. The building is to be 50 feet long and 45 feet wide and two stories high. A plan can be seen at the clerk's office on Kaskaskia." The same newspaper on November 10, 1819, recorded, "William C. Greenup, clerk, announces that the sealed bids have been received for the building of a brick Court House in Kaskaskia." G. W. Smith reports that the building cost $4,750.[10]

The Court House was one of the last buildings salvaged from old Kaskaskia as the town succumbed to the Mississippi. The materials were moved to new Kaskaskia, where it was re-erected on its original plan and stands today, though with modern windows and doors (fig. 4.7).

The Kaskaskia Land Office

The buildings that housed the Kaskaskia Land Office and later The Bank of Cairo at Kaskaskia (see next chapter) stood at the corners of Chartres and Poplar streets (fig. 4.8). The brick building was originally constructed as a private residence, but the widely spaced four chimneys and two entrances asymmetrically arranged indicate that the building was used as both a residence and office or store, each self-contained with its own entrance. While the building is generally Federal in style, the asymmetrical elements illustrate the freedom to depart from the canons of that style, which often characterized Midwestern Federal buildings. At one time this was the residence of Elias Kent Kane, who died in 1835. Later the land office and bank simultaneously occupied portions of the building before the land office transferred to a wooden frame building. By 1883, the walls of the brick building were leaning and seemed in danger of collapsing, and the photograph, taken about fifteen years later, shows

Fig. 4.6. Kaskaskia Court House at right, parochial residence at left in the distance, 1902. Courtesy of the Abraham Lincoln Presidential Library and Museum.

Fig. 4.7. Old Kaskaskia Court House rebuilt in new Kaskaskia as a schoolhouse. Photograph by MacDonald and Waters, spring 2015.

fissures in the walls (fig. 4.8).[11] The irregular slabs of limestone apparent in the street were placed so that pedestrians could cross the street in wet weather without getting muddy but so spaced that wagons could conveniently drive between them.

In the first decades of the nineteenth century, particularly after the end of the War of 1812, many immigrants moved into Illinois, some establishing farms in the countryside and others settling in new communities. There were various sorts of land claims: traditional Indian tribal rights; French, British, and American governmental land grants; and even squatter land rights. Many claims were conflicting, inexact, irregular, dubious, contradictory, or completely fraudulent. Land not subject to legitimate claims belonged to the federal government and was to be sold to settlers. The government established land offices to sort out claims and establish regular procedures for the sale of government land. The Kaskaskia Land Office was the first in Illinois. The law establishing it was passed

Fig. 4.8. Kaskaskia Land Office and Bank of Cairo at Kaskaskia,
circa 1890. From Elizabeth Holbrook, *Old 'Kaskia Days: A
Novel* (Chicago: Schulte, 1893), between pp. 24 and 25.

on March 26, 1804, but the land office was so burdened with resolving
disputed land claims that it did not begin to sell government land until
1814. In the following years, the Kaskaskia Land Office sold thousands
of acres of federal lands to settlers. Shadrach Bond served as receiver of
monies in the Kaskaskia Land Office before his term as the first governor
of the state and as registrar from 1823 until his death in 1832.[12] In 1856, the
Kaskaskia Land Office was closed and its records moved to Springfield.

The Randolph County Museum and Archives contains the standing
desk from the Kaskaskia Land Office (fig. 4.9). Titles for much of the land
in Randolph and surrounding counties passed over this desk. When a
person bought a parcel of land, the government issued a document called
a land *patent* testifying to the purchaser's ownership. The first owner of
the land was the patentee. If the land were subsequently sold by the patentee or the patentee's heirs or assignees, the legal document establishing
the sale was termed a *deed*. Prior to 1833, the president of the United
States personally signed land patents, but as western migration grew to
a flood and the federal government sold many small parcels of land to
settlers, the number of patents to be signed became overwhelming. In
1832, the commissioner of the general land office reported to Congress
that there was a backlog of over 10,500 land patents awaiting presidential

signature. The next year Congress authorized a presidential secretary to sign land patents for the president, and henceforth land patents bore the "secretarial signature" of the president's name followed with the formula "by" and the secretary's name (fig. 4.10).

The Col. Sweet Hotel

A large building, the Colonel (Col.) Sweet Hotel (figs. 4.11, 4.12), stood on Chartres Street close to the Ménard ferry. It was one of the most prominent buildings in Kaskaskia, and a number of writers made undocumented and ill-informed speculations about its age, claiming it was built

Fig. 4.9. Standing desk from the Kaskaskia Land Office, in the Randolph County Museum and Archives, Chester, Illinois. Photograph by MacDonald and Waters, summer 2015.

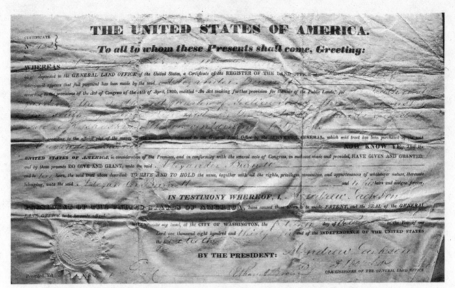

Fig. 4.10. Land patent for federal land consisting of forty acres sold to Alexander Burnett by the Kaskaskia Land Office. The deed is dated October 15, 1835, and signed for President Andrew Jackson by a secretary. The brown ink is faded but fully legible. Private collection. Used with permission.

about 1750. It is, however, absent from Pittman's 1770 plan of Kaskaskia, and the last thirty years of the eighteenth century were a time of crises and depression for Kaskaskia. It is most unlikely that such a major building was constructed then. It was probably built about 1800, at the beginning of the period of Kaskaskia's greatest prosperity. It bears some resemblance to Pierre Ménard's home, constructed about the same time, beginning in 1802. By the time the photographs were taken, the building's exterior was covered by clapboard siding, which hides most details of construction that would aid in dating, but a Federal-style fireplace, prominent in a photograph of the dining room, is an indication of an early nineteenth-century date. The houses of Pierre Ménard and Shadrach Bond, both constructed in the early nineteenth century, had similar Federal fireplaces.[13]

During its long history, this building played many roles and was known by many names. E. G. Mason writes that it was at one time the residence of Edward Coles, the second governor of Illinois.[14] It was the Col. Sweet Hotel when, in 1825, the notables of Kaskaskia feasted Lafayette there.

The building was closed and abandoned in 1833 when Pierre Ménard arranged for the sisters of the Order of the Visitation to use it for their academy and convent until a new building could be constructed for

Fig. 4.11. Col. Sweet Hotel, 1893. Photograph by Max von Fragstein, Chester, Illinois, 1893. From Elizabeth Holbrook, *Old 'Kaskia Days: A Novel* (Chicago: Schulte, 1893), between pp. 240 and 241.

Fig. 4.12. Col. Sweet Hotel, from the west, by W. G. Eggleston, September 1891. Courtesy of the Abraham Lincoln Presidential Library and Museum.

them. Later, the building was reopened as a hotel and tavern and was known variously as the Chenu House, Kaskaskia Hotel, Kaskaskia Tavern, and Union Hotel.

A newspaper account indicates the building was sixty-four feet long by thirty-six feet wide and notes, without making the construction technique at all clear, that "it was built of solid timber morticed together and bound together with heavy plates of iron" and that "the Chamber is floored with heavy timber, a custom accounted for by the fact that the early inhabitants used the upper portion of their houses for a granary."[15] A paper read before the Chicago Historical Society in 1879 indicates that the banquet room for the Lafayette dinner was "fully thirty feet square" and that one could see "beneath the porch the heavy hewn timbers of which the house is built,"[16] perhaps indicating vertical-log construction by the technique of *poteaux en terre* or *poteaux sur sol*.

INDIAN KASKASKIA

JEAN-BAPTISTE DUCOIGNE, CHIEF of the Kaskaskia, hoped that his policy of peace and cooperation with the Americans from the time of George Rogers Clark would be reciprocated, but he hoped in vain. In 1790, the newly arrived territorial governor, Arthur St. Clair, greeted Ducoigne with a compassionate speech, praising him, expressing sympathy for the sufferings of the Kaskaskia caused by other tribes, and promising support, if only vaguely. Only a few days before, St. Clair wrote to the secretary of war in Washington in a much different, dismissive tone:

> Baptiste Du Coigne, whom you may remember with the Marquis de
> Lafayette, is the chief of the Kaskaskia nation, and settled in Kas-
> kaskia. I have been plagued with a great many of his talks. The nation
> is very inconsiderable, and I do not think it necessary to trouble you
> with them at present. He himself is the greatest beggar I have met
> with among nations who are all beggars. He counts no little upon
> his having been with the American troops in Virginia, and so far he
> merits some countenance.[17]

St. Clair's generally disparaging opinion of Native Americans may have contributed to his massive defeat in 1791 by the Miami and Shawnee.

In 1792, after the defeat of the American campaigns led by Generals Harmar and St. Clair, Secretary of War Henry Knox called for a peace conference. The tribes along the Maumee River, flushed with victory, refused to attend and even killed government agents attempting to persuade them. Those tribes that came, from Illinois and around Vincennes, were not hostile to the Americans and welcomed the opportunity to air grievances against other tribes and attempt to limit growing white intrusions into their ancestral territories. Jean-Baptiste Ducoigne was the chief spokesman for the tribes, and after the conference, he along with a number of other chiefs traveled to Philadelphia, where Ducoigne met twice with Washington and had dinner with the president and other dignitaries. Ducoigne wore proudly the medal that Washington presented to him long afterward (fig. 4.13), but the conference produced no lasting results, and the Illinois Indians' situation did not improve.[18]

Contemporary estimates of the number of Kaskaskia and of Illinois Indians in general in the late eighteenth and early nineteenth centuries vary greatly, but all agree that their population had declined critically.[19] Other tribes continued to attack and kill the Illinois throughout the last decade of the eighteenth century and into the nineteenth, both in isolated incidents involving a few individuals and in major clashes. The Illinois could no longer defend their traditional territory or even effectively protect themselves, and a new American government provided no protection. As widespread alcoholism and alcohol-fueled violence

Fig. 4.13. Medal that George Washington presented to Jean-Baptiste Ducoigne in 1792. Original in Chicago History Museum.

further reduced the population and European diseases continued to take a toll, tribal unity gradually collapsed. Small bands, families, and even individuals broke off from main tribal units to live on their own, to settle with other tribes, to huddle on the fringes of white villages, or to cluster together in communities of refugees from disparate tribes on both banks of the Mississippi.[20] It seems most likely that, by 1800, the population of Indian Kaskaskia was only about a hundred,[21] and an unknown number of other tribal members were scattered widely. Even tribal names began to fall out of use. By 1800, the smaller Illinois tribes, Cahokia, Tamaroa, and Michigamea, largely disappear except in the formal language of treaties.[22] Even the collective term "Illinois" sometimes dropped out of use to be replaced by "Kaskaskia" and eventually "Peoria" as the collective designation of all surviving Illinois.

When, in 1800, Congress organized the territory of Indiana, which included Illinois, out of a portion of the Northwest Territory, William Henry Harrison became the territorial governor (fig. 4.14). Harrison's primary concern was to regulate Indian affairs and open the territory for American settlers. On August 13, 1803, Harrison and Ducoigne, along with five other Illinois, signed the Treaty of Vincennes by which the Illinois surrendered their claims to most of the land in Illinois to the United States in exchange for promises of protection.

The prologue and first two articles of the treaty describe well the beleaguered situation of the Illinois by the beginning of the nineteenth century:

A TREATY BETWEEN THE UNITED STATES OF AMERICA AND THE KASKASKIA TRIBE OF INDIANS.

Articles of a treaty made at Vincennes in the Indiana territory, between William Henry Harrison, governor of the said territory, superintendent of Indian affairs and commissioner plenipotentiary of the United States for concluding any treaty or treaties which may be found necessary with any of the Indian tribes north west of the river Ohio of the one part, and the head chiefs and warriors of the Kaskaskia tribe of Indians so called, but which tribe is the remains and rightfully represent all the tribes of the Illinois Indians, originally called the Kaskaskia, Mitchigamia, Cahokia and Tamaroi of the other part:

Fig. 4.14. Portrait of William Henry Harrison, 1813, hand-colored aquatint and etching on paper by William Strickland. National Portrait Gallery, Smithsonian Institution.

ARTICLE 1ST.

Whereas from a variety of unfortunate circumstances the several tribes of Illinois Indians are reduced to a very small number, the remains of which have been long consolidated and known by the name of the Kaskaskia tribe, and finding themselves unable to occupy the extensive tract of country which of right belongs to them and which was possessed by their ancestors for many generations, the chiefs and warriors of the said tribe being also desirous of procuring the means of improvement in the arts of civilized life, and a more certain and effectual support for their women and children, have, for the considerations hereinafter mentioned, relinquished and by these presents do relinquish and cede to the United States all the lands in the Illinois country, which the said tribe has heretofore possessed, or which they may rightfully claim, reserving to themselves however the tract of about three hundred and fifty acres near the town of Kaskaskia, which they have always held and which was secured to them by the act of Congress of the third day of March, one thousand seven hundred and ninety-one, and also the right of locating one other tract of twelve hundred and eighty acres within the bounds of that now ceded, which two tracts of land shall remain to them forever.

ARTICLE 2D.

The United States will take the Kaskaskia tribe under their immediate care and patronage, and will afford them a protection as effectual against the other Indian tribes and against all other persons whatever as is enjoyed by their own citizens. And the said Kaskaskia tribe do hereby engage to refrain from making war or giving any insult or offence to any other Indian tribe or to any foreign nation, without having first obtained the approbation and consent of the United States.[23]

In addition to the tracts of land, the Kaskaskia were to receive annually a subsidy of $1,000 in money or goods. The United States also undertook to build a house at Kaskaskia and fence a plot of one hundred acres for Ducoigne as chief, and to pay for the construction of a church and the support of a priest for the tribe. It may seem that the tribe received little in exchange for more than eight million acres of land, but in reality the Illinois merely relinquished an empty title to lands already lost.

The tribe selected an area to the south of Kaskaskia in Sand Ridge Township, Jackson County, near the Big Muddy River, as part of the land guaranteed to them by the treaty. Many of the Kaskaskia moved to this tract, and Indian Kaskaskia was reduced to just a few families. Government protection proved an empty promise. During the winter of 1804–1805, the Potawatomi raided the Kaskaskia, and in 1809 Ducoigne reported that the Kickapoo had killed his brother-in-law and stolen thirty horses.[24]

Jean-Baptiste Ducoigne lived in the house built by the government until his death in 1811,[25] after which the diminished remnant of the Kaskaskia recognized Jean-Baptiste's second son, Louis-Jefferson Ducoigne, as chief.[26] In 1818, the Illinois, including the Peoria, signed a new treaty with much the same content as the treaty of 1803.[27] This was necessary because, in 1803, the Peoria had been on the Spanish side of the Mississippi and had not signed the treaty. In 1820, a number of the Kaskaskia left Illinois, crossing the Mississippi to settle among the Peoria in Missouri. Few remained at Indian Kaskaskia, and some continued to occupy the Sand Ridge tract.

CHAPTER 5

KASKASKIA IN DECLINE, 1820–1881

FACTORS OF DECLINE

IN 1820, KASKASKIA entered a long period of decline. Losing the seat of state government to Vandalia was a major factor, but many other factors contributed as well. By 1820, the Indians who used to come with furs and hides to Kaskaskia had declined in number, and their hunting grounds were depleted. Indian trade shifted to the north and west and was increasingly dominated by a few great organizers based elsewhere, such as John Jacob Astor. By 1830, the fur trade was essentially extinct at Kaskaskia and in decline everywhere, and in 1834 the foresighted John Jacob Astor abandoned it for more attractive business opportunities.

The first steamboat came to the Mississippi River in 1811. By 1820, there were twenty on the Mississippi. In the 1830s, there were more than 1,200. Kaskaskia garnered some portion of the river trade, but the decades when the town was the entrepôt of the upper Mississippi had passed. The Kaskaskia River was inconvenient for steamboats. It required a detour off the Mississippi, and the Kaskaskia was often too shallow during the summer and icebound during the winter. Kaskaskia Landing, on the Mississippi about two miles to the west of Kaskaskia across the bottomland, became the steamboat port for the town, but St. Louis, better located and already more populous than Kaskaskia, became the economic center of the region. Nevertheless, until at least the mid-1840s, Kaskaskia remained a significant town and the home of many leading men of Illinois.

LAFAYETTE'S VISIT

IN 1825, KASKASKIA returned briefly to prominence, a moment that would long be remembered with pride. Marie-Joseph-Paul-Yves-Roche-Gilbert du Motier, marquis de Lafayette, hero of the American Revolution, came to Kaskaskia (fig. 5.1). Lafayette's grand tour of the United States in 1824–1825 was more than a sentimental journey half a century after the Revolution. The restored monarchy in France was rigidly conservative, oppressive, and opposed to Lafayette's liberal republican values. The tour was an opportunity for Lafayette to demonstrate to the French that the values of the American Revolution had made the young nation strong, prosperous, and happy. He was accompanied by, among others, a secretary, Auguste Levasseur, who was charged with recording the tour and creating a narrative that reflected Lafayette's deeply held beliefs.

Fig. 5.1. Portrait of the Marquis de Lafayette, circa 1822, oil on canvas by Ary Scheffer. National Portrait Gallery, Smithsonian Institution; gift of the John Hay Whitney Collection.

The governor of Illinois, Edward Coles, joined Lafayette's party at St. Louis. Although Lafayette's tour was behind schedule, Coles gained Lafayette's promise that he would visit Illinois, however briefly. The party decided to stop at Kaskaskia, which was on the way to his next scheduled visit, Nashville. Lafayette and his party arrived at Kaskaskia Landing in the early afternoon of April 30, 1825. Levasseur recorded that

> General Lafayette was not expected at Kaskaskia, and no preparations had been made for his unforeseen visit.[1] While we were landing, someone ran to the village, which is situated about a quarter league from the shore, and immediately returned with a coach for the General, who, in a moment after, found himself surrounded with a great number of citizens, who ran to receive him. Among the procession which was formed to accompany him, no military discipline was seen, nor the splendor of those triumphal marches which had been exhibited in the great cities, but the accents of joy and expressions of gratitude, made in this republican style, . . . proved, that wherever American liberty has extended, there are perpetuated also among the people, the love and veneration of its authors.
>
> We followed the General on foot, and arrived, almost as soon as he, at the house of General Edgar, a venerable soldier of the revolution, who received him with great kindness, and ordered that all the doors should be left open, that the citizens might share with him the pleasure of taking the hand of the adopted son of America. After a few moments had been devoted to the somewhat tumultuous expression of feeling, which the presence of the General inspired among the citizens, Governor Coles . . . approached Lafayette, around whom was drawn a close circle of Spectators, and addressed him in a feeling speech.[2]

Lafayette replied with a shorter but eloquent expression of thanks.

Lafayette spent the afternoon with General Edgar and a number of other Revolutionary War veterans and then took a brief rest. In the early evening, Lafayette, escorted by local notables, proceeded to the Col. Sweet Hotel, where a banquet in his honor had been prepared (fig. 5.2). The ladies of Kaskaskia elaborately decorated the banquet hall with flowers. The rest of the evening was occupied by a grand ball at the house of William Morrison, attended by all the notables of Kaskaskia.

In the meantime, some of Lafayette's party had wandered about the town, conversing with French Canadians and Indians and then crossing

Fig. 5.2. Room in which Lafayette dined, sadly deteriorated by the
time the photograph was taken by Max von Fragstein of Chester,
Illinois, in 1893. From Elizabeth Holbrook, *Old 'Kaskia Days: A
Novel* (Chicago: Schulte, 1893), between pp. 280 and 281.

the Kaskaskia River to visit an Indian encampment. Upon returning to
Kaskaskia, one of the party informed Levasseur that he had met a young
Indian woman, Marie, daughter of the deceased chief of the Kaskaskia who
had fought beside Lafayette during the Revolution. Levasseur introduced
Marie to Lafayette, who left the ball to spent time with her. Marie showed
Lafayette the letter of commendation that he had presented to her father
in 1778, her father's most precious possession, given to her at his death.[3]
Late that evening Lafayette departed from Kaskaskia by steamboat.

THE LAST OF THE KASKASKIA IN ILLINOIS

AFTER THE DEPARTURE of Lafayette, Kaskaskia returned to its sleepy
existence. By 1832, Louis Ducoigne, chief of the few remaining members
of the Kaskaskia tribe, had died, and in that year the Kaskaskia and Peoria
signed yet another treaty by which they relinquished their few remaining
landholdings in Illinois and Missouri, with the exception of the 350 acres
on which Indian Kaskaskia was located. That plot was reserved for Ellen
Ducoigne, daughter of Louis Ducoigne. In exchange, the Kaskaskia and
Peoria were to receive "one hundred and fifty sections of land . . . west of

the State of Missouri, on the waters of the Osage River," in what would become the state of Kansas.[4]

This was the end of Indian Kaskaskia and the Kaskaskia Indians in Illinois. The last Kaskaskia officially left Illinois in 1833, aided by Pierre Ménard, who arranged passage for them on a steamboat. By 1850, even Ellen Ducoigne had left Illinois for Indian Territory.[5] Yet, oral traditions in several Illinois towns, difficult to document, maintain that a few never left, found work on farms, gradually acquired their own plots of land, and in the course of several generations integrated themselves into local communities.

THE CONVENT OF THE VISITATION

IN THE SPRING of 1833, eight sisters of the Order of the Visitation of Holy Mary came from Georgetown, DC, at the invitation of Bishop Joseph Rosati of St. Louis to establish a convent and school for girls at Kaskaskia. The people of Kaskaskia were unprepared for their arrival. The bishop had been unable to send notice of their coming because St. Louis was under quarantine due to cholera.[6]

Fig. 5.3. Sketch by Mrs. H. S. Currie, circa 1865, bearing an inscription: "Old Visitation Convent. This Convent was built by Col. Menard. Vacated in 1844. The sisters leaving the building during the flood. The water reached second story." Courtesy of the Abraham Lincoln Presidential Library and Museum.

The sisters' first impressions of Kaskaskia were not good, but a leading citizen, William Morrison, took the situation in hand and extended hospitality, and Pierre Ménard, with typical generosity, aided the sisters. Ménard first turned over his old store to the sisters, but it quickly became apparent that the store was too small. Ménard then arranged for them to begin their school for girls and young women in the building that had been known by many names: Kaskaskia Tavern, Chenu House, Union Hotel, and the Col. Sweet Hotel (see figs. 4.11, 4.12). Sister Josephine Barber wrote, "we had the counter removed from the barroom which was in the future to serve the triple purpose of refectory, play room, and class room for the children."[7] They resided in these improvised quarters until a new building, financed by Pierre Ménard, was completed three years later.

The new building consisted of the school and an attached convent. The school, named the Ménard Young Ladies' Academy, was a four-story Federal-style brick building 110 feet long by 32 feet wide (fig. 5.3). Bricks were first made at Kaskaskia for its construction. The convent

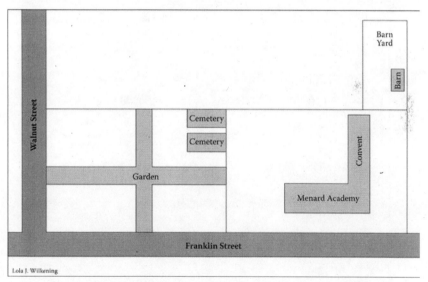

Fig. 5.4. Plan of Ménard Young Ladies' Academy, Convent of the Visitation, and grounds. By MacDonald and Waters, derived from William Barnaby Faherty, *Deep Roots and Golden Wings: One Hundred and Fifty Years with the Visitation Sisters in the Archdiocese of Saint Louis, 1833 to 1983* (St. Louis: River City, 1982), 30; and *An Illustrated Historical Atlas Map of Randolph County, Ills.* ([Edwardsville?], IL: W. R Brink, 1875), plate 25.

YOUNG LADIES' ACADEMY OF THE VISITATION,
AT KASKASKIA, ILLINOIS.

M. Ellen Flannigan, *Superieur*.

The situation of this academy is near the village of Kaskaskia, commanding on one side a full view of the beautiful river of the same name, as it winds; its course beneath a ridge of lofty hills, and on the other overlooking a considerable portion of the village.

PLAN OF INSTRUCTION.

The course of instruction, commencing with the elements of an English Education, embraces—Orthography, Reading, Writing, Arithmetic, English and French Grammar and Composition, Geography, Sacred and Profane History, Ancient and Modern Chronology, Mythology, Poetical Composition, Rhetoric, Philosophy, Chemistry, Astronomy, use of the Maps and Globes. Also—Music, Vocal and Instrumental, on the Harp, Piano and Guitar; Painting in Water Colors and on Velvet; Plain and Ornamental Needle-work, Tapestry, Lace and Bead-work, &c.

TERMS.

Board and tuition, - - - -	$125 00	per annum.
Tuition alone for day scholars, -	- 24 00	"
Paper, quills and ink, - - -	4 00	"

EXTRA CHARGES.

French Language, quarterly, -	$5 00	per annum.
Drawing and Painting on Velvet, -	5 00	"
Harp and its use, - - - -	16 00	"
Piano, - - - - - -	12 00	"
Guitar, - - - - - - -	- 6 00	"
Medical attendance, - - - -	75	"
Mending of clothes, if done at the institution,	1 00	"
Bed and bedding, unless furnished by the parents,	1 75	"

N. B. Boarders are requested to pay semi-annually, and day-scholars quarterly in advance.

When in sickness extraordinary expenses are incurred, a bill of the same will be presented.

There are at present 70 pupils in the academy, 50 of whom are boarders. There are also 12 orphans in the house.

Fig. 5.5. Prospectus for Ménard Young Ladies' Academy, 1838. From Fielding Lucas Jr., ed., *The Metropolitan Catholic Almanac and Laity's Directory for the Year of Our Lord 1839* (Baltimore: published by the author, 1838), 147–48.

was an attached wing built of wood, two stories high and 150 feet long. The two parts together constituted the largest building in Kaskaskia and cost $30,000, an immense sum at the time. There were also several outbuildings, a barn, a garden, and a small cemetery (fig. 5.4).

The school was an immediate success and prospered. Sophie Ménard was the first graduate, in 1838. A prospectus for the academy published that year describes the plan of instruction and charges (fig. 5.5). Some parents paid tuition in goods and services rather than cash, which was universally scarce in the Midwest, especially after the national financial panic of 1837. Pierre Ménard paid for his children and grandchildren, for the children of friends short of funds, and for orphans. Pierre Ménard's and his wife's frequent charitable works were done privately, without display or publicity. In 1841, Bishop Kenrick of St. Louis prevailed upon six of the sisters to leave Kaskaskia to establish another convent and school in St. Louis.

THE NEW BRICK CHURCH

IN 1838, A main support beam of the Church of the Immaculate Conception broke, and the building partially collapsed. The people of Kaskaskia had erected the old vertical-log building in 1775, just sixty-three years previously, but architectural styles had changed so greatly during the intervening years that visitors to Kaskaskia saw the old French vertical-log construction as strange and antique. The community decided to erect a new church of modern French design, an austere rectangular building made of brick, which had been available locally since the construction of the Ménard academy a few years earlier. Subsequently, after 1860, a steeple was added to the front of the building in a contrasting early Gothic style (fig. 5.6).

THE BANK OF CAIRO AT KASKASKIA

DURING THE FIRST decades of the nineteenth century, migrants increasingly flooded into Illinois and other midwestern states, where farmland could be purchased from federal land offices for a modest sum per acre. Many who wanted land, however, lacked ready cash, which was in short supply but high demand. Not only did land purchases require financing, but other ventures did as well, such as the construction of canals,

Fig. 5.6. Earliest photograph of the brick Church of the Immaculate
Conception and the parochial residence. A notation indicates it was
taken about 1878. Original print in the Chester Public Library.

establishment of new towns, and fur trading expeditions to the west.
The demand for ready capital led to the establishment of private banks.
W. H. Crawford, US secretary of the treasury, explained in a report of
February 24, 1820, that "banks have been incorporated, not because
there was capital seeking investment; not because the places where they
were established had commerce and manufactures which required their
fostering aid; but because men without active capital wanted the means
of obtaining loans."[8]

In theory, members of the public would pool their resources by investing in the bank, which would lend money to sound ventures, such
as to syndicates that would purchase large tracts of government land to
resell in smaller tracts to individual farmers on long-term mortgages.
Farmers who did not have the cash to purchase land directly from the
government would be able to get land, and the interest on their loans
would accrue to the bank's investors, while furthering the development
of the community where the bank was established. G. W. Dowrie provided a more succinct and cynical evaluation: "An apt appraisal current
at that time was that the chief function of a western bank was to manufacture and issue paper money on easy terms to the ambitious and
gullible inhabitants."[9]

The issuance of paper money by private banks did increase the amount of money in circulation and stimulate the economy, but the banks had a frequently fatal weakness. The territorial legislature and later the State of Illinois chartered banks but neither guaranteed the banks nor the paper money they issued. Banks could only offer as assurance their own resources, tangible and intangible. Tangible resources consisted of capital from the sale of shares in the bank, interest earned from loans, and profits from investments in land or development projects. These seldom equaled in worth the paper money issued by a bank. Consequently, banks also relied on intangible assets, such as faith in the bank directors, anticipated interest earned on loans, anticipated profits from the sale of bank-owned assets, and the growth of communities and the banks serving them.

Banks often functioned well during times of national prosperity and economic stability, but if borrowers defaulted on repaying their loans, investments failed to prosper, or anticipated growth was not realized, a bank would be unable to redeem its paper money for hard currency, gold and silver coins. Great and abrupt changes in the national money supply and credit, which occurred at irregular intervals throughout the first half of the nineteenth century, also disrupted banking and undermined public confidence. Such changes could and did destroy even well-managed banks.

Banks often competed ruthlessly with one another, both within their own states and with banks in neighboring states. Banks used political connections to get the federal and state governments to deposit funds from land sales with them rather than with competitors. Banks sometimes refused to accept the paper money issued by other banks or accepted it only at a discounted rate. Banks spread rumors about the financial status of other banks and even gathered substantial sums of paper money issued by other banks to present suddenly and demand be redeemed in gold or silver, with the hope of embarrassing the issuing bank and destroying public trust.

In 1816, the territorial legislature chartered the first bank in Illinois, The Bank of Illinois at Shawneetown. Shawneetown was a hub for the land and water routes, the site of a US land office, and a small but active center of trade. Other banks soon followed. In 1818, the state issued charters for The Bank of Kaskaskia, The Bank of Edwardsville, and The Bank of Cairo. The Bank of Illinois at Shawneetown suspended operations in 1823, although the charter was not revoked, and the bank reopened in 1834 but went out of business in 1842. The Bank of Kaskaskia failed to sell sufficient stock and never opened. The Bank of Edwardsville collapsed in 1821.

The Bank of Cairo had a more complex history.[10] Shortly after the state granted a charter to the City and Bank Company of Cairo, the chief promoter died suddenly and the corporation collapsed. The Bank of Cairo failed to open, and a different corporation, the Cairo City and Canal Company, finally established the town of Cairo in 1836–1837. Although The Bank of Cairo did not open, its charter remained valid. The state constitution, ratified in 1819, provided for the establishment of a state bank and prohibited any other banks to operate in Illinois, with the exception of those already chartered. In 1835, a group of investors took advantage of this exception to renew the charter of The Bank of Cairo, which was finally opened as The Bank of Cairo at Kaskaskia, but there never was a Bank of Cairo at Cairo. The bank first occupied a portion of the same brick building as the Kaskaskia Land Office, an indication of the close relationship between bank financing and land sales, and later the land office moved to a wood-frame building across the street from the bank (see fig. 4.8).

Fig. 5.7. Unissued "specimen" one-dollar note of the Bank of Cairo at Kaskaskia. Such notes, rendered invalid by the absence of signatures, number, and date and by the presence of punched holes, were kept as references by the printer and the bank. The central vignette shows allegorical figures of agriculture, manufacturing, and commerce hailing a trading ship. Photograph courtesy of Heritage Auctions.

The Bank of Cairo at Kaskaskia initially operated conservatively and successfully, and it provided many of the low-denomination banknotes of twenty dollars or less in circulation within Illinois from 1839 until shortly before its failure. The bank issued currency in denominations of $1, $2, $3, $5, $10, and $20; the plates were engraved and the banknotes printed by the firm of Underwood, Bald, Spencer, and Huffy of New York and Philadelphia.[11] The same firm printed $50 and $100 notes for the bank, but they seem not to have been issued.[12] This was one of a number of firms that produced high-quality counterfeit-resistant notes for a variety of banks. A bank could select vignettes, decorations, and typefaces from the company's stock. The vignettes did not depict local realities, although they might reflect aspirations. All of the banknotes were printed on only one side (figs. 5.7, 5.8).

Two events drove The Bank of Cairo at Kaskaskia into bankruptcy. In 1842, the state government, distrusting the growing flood of paper money from poorly financed banks and seeking to promote its own banking scheme, refused to accept the notes of any private banks in the payment of taxes, licensing fees, and all other monies due to the government. About the same time, the Cairo City and Canal Company, in which the bank's officers had invested heavily, collapsed. The bank went into bankruptcy in 1842, and its charter was revoked in 1843.

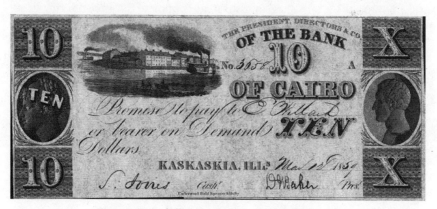

Fig. 5.8. Ten-dollar note of the Bank of Cairo at Kaskaskia, issued on March 12, 1839, numbered and signed by the cashier and bank president. The central vignette depicts an imaginary view of an industrial riverfront town, in no way reflective of the reality of Kaskaskia. Photograph courtesy of Heritage Auctions.

IMPRESSIONS OF KASKASKIA IN
THE 1830S AND 1840S

EDMUND FLAGG TOURED the West in the 1830s and wrote a flamboyant, highly romanticized account for the eastern reading public, including his impressions of Kaskaskia:[13]

There is, however, one beautiful and extensive farm under high cultivation nearly opposite Kaskaskia, which no traveler can fail to observe and admire. It is the residence of Colonel M—,[14] a French gentleman of wealth, who has done everything a cultivated taste could dictate to render it a delightful spot. A fine, airy farmhouse stands beneath the bluffs, built after the French style, with heavy roof, broad balconies, and with a rare luxury in this region—green Venetian blinds. The outhouses, most of them substantially constructed of stone, are surpassed in beauty and extent only by the residence itself. Fields yellow with golden harvest, orchards loaded with fruit, and groves, and parks, and pastures sprinkled with grazing cattle, spread out themselves on every side. In the back-ground rise the wooded bluffs, gracefully rounded to their summits, while in front roams the gentle Kaskaskia, beyond which, peacefully reposing in the sunlight, lay the place of my destination . . . drawing nigh to the eastern shore of the stream opposite the ancient French village Kaskaskia. The sun was going down, and as I approached the sandy edge of the sea-green water, a gay bevy of young folks were whirling the long, narrow, skiff-like ferry-boat like a bird across the stream, by means of a hawser to which it was attached, and which extended from shore to shore. In my own turn I stepped into the boat, and in a few moments the old French negro had forced it half across the river, at this spot about three or four hundred yards in width.[15] For one who has ever visited Kaskaskia in the last beautiful days of summer, a pen like my own need hardly be employed to delineate the loveliness of the scene which now opened upon the view. For miles the gleamy surface of the gentle Kaskaskia might be seen retreating from the eye, till lost at length in its windings through the forests of its banks, resting their deep shadows on the stream in all the calm magnificence of inanimate nature. The shore I was leaving swelled gracefully up from the water's edge, clothed in forests until it reached the bluffs, which towered abrupt and loftily; while here and there along the landscape the low roof of a log cabin could be caught peeping forth from the dark shrubbery. The bank of the stream I was approaching presented an aspect entirely the reverse; less lovely, but more picturesque. A low sandy beach stretched itself more than a mile along the river, destitute of trees, and rounding itself gently away into a broad green plain. Upon this plain . . . at the distance of a few hundred yards from the river is situated all that now remains of "old Kaskaskia." From the centre rises a tall Gothic spire, hoary with time, surmounted by an iron cross;[16] and around this nucleus are clustered irregularly, at various intervals, the heavy-roofed, time-stained cottages of the French inhabitants. These houses are usually like those of the West India planters, but a single story in height—and the surface which they occupy is, of course, in the larger class, proportionably increased. They are con-structed, some of rough limestone, some of timber, framed in ev-ery variety of position—horizontal, perpendicular, oblique, or all united—thus retaining their shape till they rot to the ground, with the interstices stuffed with the fragments of stone, and the exter-nal surface stuccoed with mortar; others—a few only—are framed, boarded, etc., in modern style. Nearly all have galleries in front, some of them spacious, running around the whole building, and all have garden-plats enclosed by stone walls or stoccades. Some of these curious-looking structures are old, have bided the storm-winds of more than a century. It is this circumstance which throws over the place that antiquated, venerable aspect to which I have alluded.

A few years later, in 1841, J. C. Wild published the first view of Kaskaskia in a collection of views depicting towns of the Mississippi Valley (fig. 5.9). The view is from the bluff on the eastern side of the Kaskaskia River, looking toward the west. The distant tree line marks the course of the Mississippi. Pierre Ménard's rope ferry and a short-lived bridge are visible on the Kaskaskia River. The first bridge over the Kaskaskia was in the process of being erected in 1822, when it was carried away by a flood. It was rebuilt, but it proved unprofitable and so went out of use about 1828. Construction of the second and last bridge in original Kaskaskia commenced in 1840 and was still not complete when it collapsed in 1843.[17] The Convent of the Visitation

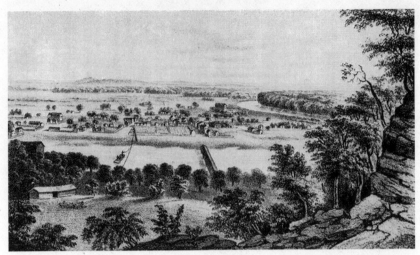

Fig. 5.9. View of Kaskaskia, 1841. Lithograph by J. C. Wild, from J. C. Wild
and L. F. Thomas, *The Valley of the Mississippi Illustrated in a Series of
Views* (St. Louis: Chambers and Knapp, 1841), plate 13, opposite p. 61.

is the large building at the far right of the town near the bend in the
river. Kaskaskia was not compactly built. Some of the many open
spaces in Kaskaskia were used as gardens or stockyards; others were
apparently just empty lots.

A second view of the city is copied from the Wild lithograph (fig. 5.10).
Although Joseph Meyer claimed the views in *Meyer's Universum* were
original works prepared just for the publication, it is apparent that this
engraving of Kaskaskia, made about 1850, is derived from Wild's 1841
view; the bridge across the Kaskaskia River collapsed in 1843 and was not
replaced. The engraving is less reliable than Wild's original. The engraver
has added buildings along the riverbank and elsewhere at random. The
view is rendered more romantic by the substitution of a rustic cabin in
the left foreground for the rather nondescript shed in the original, by the
exaggeration of the distant hills in the background, and by the addition
of dramatic clouds. The engraving appeared in a number of editions of
Meyer's Universum published after 1850.[18]

THE GREAT FLOOD OF 1844

IN 1844, DISASTER struck Kaskaskia. Ferdinand Maxwell, the city clerk,
wrote a direct, sober account:

Fig. 5.10. View of Kaskaskia. Engraving from J. Meyer, *Meyer's Universum*, 18 (Hildburghausen: Verlag des Bibliographischen Instituts, 1857), following p. 156.

This day, June 28th, A.D. 1844, I have witnessed the whole of the town of Kaskaskia inundated by the high water, some seven feet upon an average. The whole population of the place removed over on the hills or highlands opposite, and a great many took shelter at Col. Pierre Menard's house. . . . Many houses were carried off by the water; the water commenced rising about the 12th of June and commenced falling about five o'clock, P.M., this 28th day of June. Given under my hand,

F. Maxwell, Clerk[19]

Buildings were ruined, swept off their foundations, basements collapsed. Some homes disappeared entirely, and others were left wracked, twisted, and uninhabitable. One newspaper reported the destruction of another:

The proprietor of the "[Kaskaskia] Republican" was busily engaged in rendering assistance to families in making their escape, and whilst so engaged the cellar walls of his printing office gave way, and the house sunk to the water. His press, type, materials, furniture, books, papers and files were all buried twelve to fifteen feet deep in water. . . . The scene in Kaskaskia is represented as being one of complete ruin.[20]

Shortly before the flood, the Catholic Church had reorganized the diocese of St. Louis, dividing it in two, and Bishop Kenrick traveled to Kaskaskia with the new bishop to introduce him to the sisters. They arrived to find the school and convent inundated to the second story. A singular scene ensued as two bishops, priests, and steamboat stevedores labored side by side to load the sisters and students as well as furniture and all manner of goods (pianos, harps, books, desks, benches) into the steamboat, tethered to the half-submerged convent. The boat then moved to the Ménard house, where many refugees from the flooded town had gathered. After a brief respite, Captain Ludwig of the steamboat *Indiana* carried bishops, sisters, students, and goods to St. Louis, where the sisters and students joined their brethren. The convent was never reoccupied by the sisters after the flood of 1844, though it seems to have been occasionally used by squatters. The academy was eventually demolished to salvage the bricks it contained, at least some of which were used to build a parochial residence at Kaskaskia.[21]

KASKASKIA AFTER 1844

AFTER THE WATER receded, Kaskaskia was struck by a deadly epidemic, probably the result of a general contamination of wells by the runoff from privies and pastures. Rather than rebuild in Kaskaskia, many people and businesses left the town. Some, like the nuns, went to St. Louis. Noted jurist Nathaniel Pope moved to Alton. Many moved to Chester, founded in 1829, about six miles south of Kaskaskia, a little downriver from the confluence of the Kaskaskia and Mississippi. Chester had also been badly damaged by the flood, but the low part of town was backed by bluffs, where some of it had escaped the flood and where new homes and businesses could be built high above any potential flood.

Other towns saw the devastation of Kaskaskia as an opportunity to move the county seat. In 1847, the Illinois General Assembly passed a bill calling for three elections to determine the seat of Randolph County. The first election included all towns in contention. The campaign leading to the election was bitter and the election itself fraudulent. Chester garnered the most votes, Sparta second, and Kaskaskia third. Evansville and Centre, fourth and fifth, were eliminated. The second round of voting, yet more rancorous and crooked, eliminated Kaskaskia. The third election, exceedingly acrimonious and underhanded, gave the county seat to Chester. The citizens of Sparta and Kaskaskia were outraged, even though they were equally involved in election fraud.[22]

Henceforth, Chester assumed the dominant role in both government and business in Randolph County, and Kaskaskia continued to dwindle. In 1856, the Kaskaskia Land Office, open since 1804, transferred its files to the Springfield Land District Office and closed its doors. Other than its architectural heritage of Franco-American and large Federal buildings, Kaskaskia came to resemble many other midwestern farm towns. There was little new construction.

In 1875, W. R. Brink and Company published *An Illustrated Historical Atlas Map of Randolph County, Ills.*[23] containing the first published plan of the town since Pittman's map of 1770. The village was more regular in 1875 than a century earlier, but its basic form remained recognizable (fig. 5.11). A modification of the 1875 map is stripped of the lot numbers and shows the location of additional buildings and graveyards (fig. 5.12).

In 1877, members of the Missouri Historical Society visited Kaskaskia. Accompanying them was the prominent St. Louis photographer John A. Scholten. The visit and Scholten's participation were described in the

Fig. 5.11. Map of Kaskaskia, 1875. From *An Illustrated Historical Atlas Map of Randolph County, Ills.* ([Edwardsville?], IL: W. R Brink, 1875), portion of plate 25.

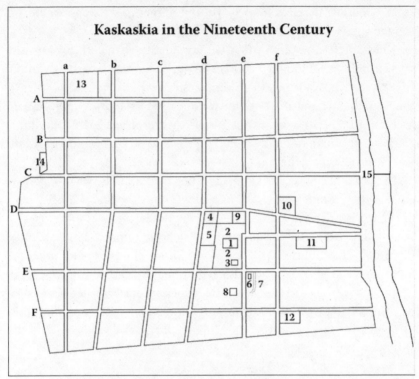

Fig. 5.12. Modified map of Kaskaskia, circa 1875. *Key to Kaskaskia locations in the nineteenth century*: *1*, Church of the Immaculate Conception. *2*, Catholic cemeteries. *3*, Parochial residence. *4*, William Morrison's house. *5*, William Morrison's garden. *6*, *Poteaux sur sol* cabin. *7*, Farm lane. *8*, Court House. *9*, Territorial and State House. *10*, General Edgar's house. *11*, Jesuit compound, later British Fort Gage. *12*, Masonic cemetery. *13*, Convent of the Visitation. *14*, Protestant church and cemetery. *15*, Ménard ferry. *East-west streets*: *A*, Franklin St. *B*, Independence St. *C*, Chartres St. *D*, Elm St. *E*, Pecan St. *F*, Republican St. *North-south streets*: *a*, Walnut St. *b*, Indian St. *c*, Persimmon St. *d*, Poplar St. *e*, Church Alley. *f*, Pear St. Based on *An Illustrated Historical Atlas Map of Randolph County, Ills.*, portion of plate 25.

St. Louis Republican (July 19, 1877) and reprinted in the *Fair Play* (Ste. Geneviève, MO, August 2, 1877). Scholten made photographs during this trip,[24] which apparently have not survived, but an unsigned short article in *Frank Leslie's Illustrated Newspaper* includes an engraving derived from one of Scholten's photographs (fig. 5.13). The view is from the north looking south. The engraving inaccurately depicts the church tower, which was attached to the front of the building and of a different style

Fig. 5.13. Illustration of Kaskaskia. Derived from a photograph by the St. Louis photographer John A. Scholten, in Frank Leslie, ed., "Kaskaskia, the Old French Capital of Illinois," *Frank Leslie's Illustrated Newspaper*, October 27, 1877, 125.

than shown in the engraving. Still, the view gives a good impression of the appearance of the town, the intermingling of small and large homes, shops, sheds, gardens, stables, and many open spaces.

On July 4, 1878, visitors gathered in Kaskaskia to commemorate the hundredth anniversary of George Rogers Clark's bloodless capture of Illinois. A postcard published long afterward depicts the town as seen on that occasion. The lithographic image was probably made from a photograph; typically such images were manipulated for clarity, so details cannot be assumed to be accurate. In this case, the church tower is certainly not correctly depicted (fig. 5.14). The large building at the far

Fig. 5.14. Postcard view of Kaskaskia, July 4, 1878. Creator, Curt Teich & Co.; Publisher, W. L. Hylton, Chester, 1937.

left of the image is the Kaskaskia Court House. To the left of the church is the parochial residence. To the right of the church is Elm Street with its array of large Midwestern Federal houses, and further to the right is the Ménard rope ferry at the base of Chartres Street. The 1878 image shows a smaller Kaskaskia than the 1841 image (see fig. 5.9), and by 1841 Kaskaskia was already much small than at its greatest, about 1820.

Gradually, as the population diminished during the second half of the nineteenth century, some buildings were reused for new purposes. Kaskaskia Court House became the village school and then later a storehouse for grain. A tiny jail was sufficient for the reduced community (fig. 5.15). Some buildings were simply abandoned as the population declined.

The first recorded expressions that Kaskaskia suffered under a curse were written in the 1830s and 1840s. Father Benedict Roux suggested the origin of the concept lay in a statement that Father Pierre Gibault made in the late eighteenth century, but in the 1840s the concept of the curse remained vague, unconnected with any narrative account of events.[25]

Fig. 5.15. Kaskaskia jail, circa 1890. Photograph in
the Missouri History Museum, St. Louis.

CHAPTER 6

DESTRUCTION, 1881–CIRCA 1913

IN THE MID-1860S, a silent change presaged the destruction of Kaskaskia: the Mississippi river began to shift its bed. In the thousands of years since the last ice age, the Mississippi had often changed course, but in the nineteenth century, human activity greatly magnified the power of the Mississippi to alter the landscape quickly. Prior to the nineteenth century, the banks of the Mississippi and the other large rivers of Illinois were lined with mixed deciduous trees and a thick undergrowth of brush and vines. The tangled vegetal mass slowed floodwaters, and roots anchored the soil. The Indian and French populations were small and scarcely changed the riverbank vegetation except in a few small, scattered places. Then, in the nineteenth century, the population increased greatly. The settlers cut wood for cabins and for heating, fencing, and endeavors such as making salt, which they produced in large quantities on the small Saline River near its confluence with the Mississippi near Kaskaskia.

The side-wheel and stern-wheel steamboats played an even greater role in denuding the banks of the Mississippi. The wood requirements of the steam engines were enormous. Boats of average size burned twenty-five cords of wood a day, and the largest steamboats of the mid-nineteenth century consumed three times as much.[1] Woodcutters bought permission from landowners to harvest the trees that lined the riverbanks. They cut, sized, and stacked the logs for sale to passing steamers, and after the wood in one area was exhausted, the woodcutters moved to the next. In Illinois, where the trees were often limited to a belt along the river, the stripping of the riverbanks was particularly severe. Trees and thickets of brush and vines no longer anchored the soil; riverbanks eroded and collapsed. The shape of the river changed, growing wider and shallower. Erosion was particularly severe at bends.

John Howard Burnham witnessed the beginning of the change that would destroy Kaskaskia. He recalled that when, as a member of the Union army he had traveled down the Mississippi in 1863, there was a good steamboat landing at Ste. Geneviève; but when he passed by on a steamboat in late 1867, "the river channel had then moved away from the town" and his boat grounded in shoaling water.[2] The current had shifted toward the neck of land that separated the Mississippi from the Kaskaskia River, and in the coming years the Mississippi rapidly ate away the bank north of Kaskaskia (fig. 6.1).

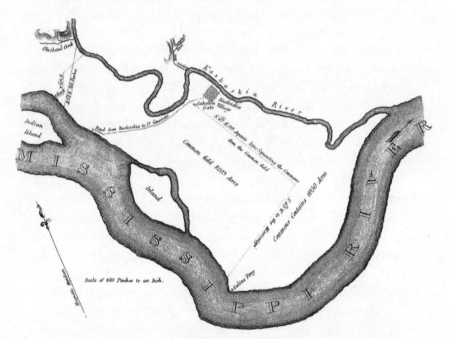

Fig. 6.1. Map of the Mississippi near Kaskaskia before the Mississippi began to encroach on the neck of land separating it from the Kaskaskia River. *Village Tract and Common Field of Kaskaskia Village* by county surveyor David C. Robinson, 1807, published in "Report of Albert Gallatin, Secretary of the Treasury, December 31, 1810, on Land Claims in the District of Kaskaskia, Communicated to the Senate on January 2, 1811, in Conformity with Acts of March 26, 1804, and March 3, 1805," in Walter Lowrie, *American State Papers*, vol. 8: *Public Lands*, vol. 2 (Washington: Duff Green, 1834), facing p. 148. Ex. Doc. 180. 11th Congress. 2nd Session.

As the Mississippi encroached on the smaller Kaskaskia River during the late 1870s, the federal Mississippi River Commission erected substantial constructions to slow the current and prevent erosion of the narrowing neck of land between the two rivers, but the Mississippi rendered all such efforts in vain. The winter of 1880–1881 was harsh. Snow was heavy in the northern part of the Mississippi watershed, and the Mississippi was covered with ice as far south as Cairo, approaching two feet in thickness at St. Louis. In February, an early thaw upriver caused the Mississippi at St. Louis to rise eight feet in a single day. The high water broke the ice into massive blocks, which piled up one on another and swept downstream, tearing away the banks and man-made obstacles. In April, the Mississippi first flowed into the Kaskaskia River above the town (fig. 6.2).[3]

When the level of the Mississippi dropped, water stopped pouring over the neck of land between the two rivers. During the next few years, the Mississippi discharged into the Kaskaskia only intermittently during high water. But each time it did, the water eroded the earth and cut the neck even lower, until by the mid-1880s the Mississippi began flowing continually into the Kaskaskia River.[4] The bed of the Kaskaskia River could not accommodate the inflow from the Mississippi. The east bank of the Kaskaskia in this area consisted of limestone bluffs, highly resistant to erosion, but the west bank, on which the town of Kaskaskia was situated, was composed of poorly consolidated, easily eroded alluvial deposits.

As the Mississippi widened the riverbed, it destroyed Kaskaskia. The Mississippi claimed some outlying buildings soon after the breakthrough in 1881, but most of Kaskaskia collapsed into the river, building by building, over the next twenty-five years, not without danger to the inhabitants. The owner of Beiter's Drug Store disappeared, leaving behind a family on the same day that a substantial part of the river embankment collapsed into the Mississippi (fig. 6.3). He was never seen again.[5]

As the river ate away Kaskaskia, the citizens salvaged what they could. They carried away doors, windows, and anything else useful from doomed structures. A few brick and stone buildings were completely dissembled and the materials hauled off before the river could swallow them, but most simply crumbled into the river and were swept away (fig. 6.4).

By 1892, the Mississippi threatened the Church of the Immaculate Conception and the three cemeteries in Kaskaskia, the Catholic, Protestant, and Masonic. The Catholic was, of course, much the oldest. Few graves were marked before the late eighteenth century, when iron-cross

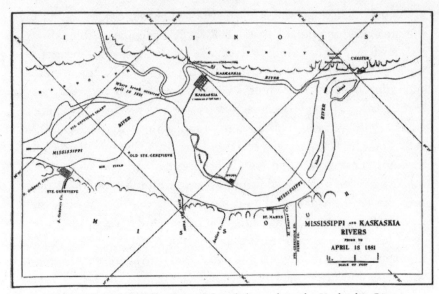

Fig. 6.2. Map of the Mississippi's breakthrough to the Kaskaskia River, April 1881. From J. H. Burnham, "Destruction of Kaskaskia by the Mississippi River," *Transactions of the Illinois State Historical Society*, 1914, facing p. 103.

Fig. 6.3. Beiter's Drug Store, Kaskaskia, circa 1890. Print in the Missouri History Museum, St. Louis.

Fig. 6.4. Large building collapsing into the widening channel of the Mississippi. Courtesy of the Abraham Lincoln Presidential Library and Museum.

Fig. 6.5. Iron-cross grave marker from a French colonial cemetery in Kaskaskia. Missouri History Museum, St. Louis. http://mohistory.org/search?text=Kaskaskia%20cemetery&type=collection%20item.v

grave markers became common, at least for the wealthier members of the community. One of the distinctively French-style grave markers from Kaskaskia survives in the Missouri History Museum (fig. 6.5). Gravestones became common in the nineteenth century. The Kaskaskia churchyard must have appeared much like the surviving cemeteries of Prairie du Rocher (fig. 6.6) and Old Mines, Missouri.

The state took action to move the graves from the Kaskaskia cemeteries across to Garrison Hill, near the earthworks of old Fort Kaskaskia.

Fig. 6.6. Prairie du Rocher Cemetery. Photograph
by MacDonald and Waters, spring 2015.

Fig. 6.7. Garrison Hill Cemetery. Beyond the trees is the
Mississippi, which flows where Kaskaskia once stood. Photo
by David Ramsey, late winter 2015; used with permission.

Some five thousand graves, along with a number of gravestones, were moved but not without controversy. Some argued that the graves should not be disturbed by man and that the Mississippi be allowed to take its course. Others found fault with the expenses involved and the maintenance of the Garrison Hill Cemetery after its establishment. In time, however, the cemetery became and remains a beautiful memorial to the early pioneers of Illinois and citizens of Kaskaskia (fig. 6.7).

In 1893, the parishioners bowed to necessity, tore down the brick Church of the Immaculate Conception and salvaged the building materials to construct a church at new Kaskaskia. The process was completed in the first days of 1894. A photograph taken as the demolition began records the appearance of the church on the eve of its destruction (figs. 6.8, 6.9).

A newspaper article reported the demolition: "The church contained 350,000 brick, which were hauled away by forty teams voluntarily sent to the ruined building by devout farmers in the vicinity. The material is being used again in the construction of a new church upon a higher point of land about two miles distant, where it is thought the erosion of the river banks will not disturb it."[6] The parochial residence was also partially demolished for its materials and re-erected in new Kaskaskia. A late photograph shows the rear wing of the residence, which was not salvaged, in a state of partial collapse (fig. 6.10).

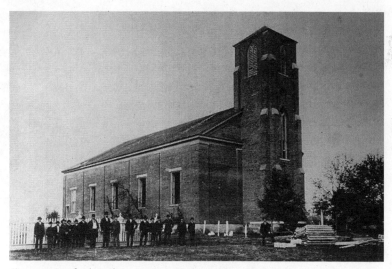

Fig. 6.8. Brick church in 1893 on the eve of its demolition. Windows have been removed and piled before the front of the building. Photograph, probably by Max von Fragstein, in the Randolph County Museum.

Fig. 6.9. Interior of the brick church, 1893. Photo by Max von Fragstein; courtesy of the Abraham Lincoln Presidential Library and Museum.

Fig. 6.10. Back wing of the parochial residence, partially collapsed. The label "1." at center right marks collapsed foundations. Photograph by Valentine Smith, January 1906; print in the Chicago History Museum.

Fig. 6.11. Panorama of Kaskaskia, 1893. By Max von Fragstein, photographer from Chester, Illinois. Courtesy of the Abraham Lincoln Presidential Library and Museum.

Fig. 6.12. Panorama of Kaskaskia, 1895. From H. W. Beckwith, "General George Roger Clark's Conquest of the Illinois," in *Collections of the Illinois State Historical Library*, vol. 1 (Springfield: H. W. Rokker, 1903), following p. 200.

As the historic old town crumbled, and one after another edifice disappeared, authors penned novels about life in Kaskaskia, manifesting a sense of loss and nostalgia. Photographers recorded panoramas of the shrinking town, street scenes, buildings, and the devastation wrought by the river (figs. 6.11–6.13).[7]

Fig. 6.13. Territorial and State House partially collapsed into the Mississippi, 1900. Courtesy of the Abraham Lincoln Presidential Library and Museum.

Fig. 6.14. "Mule Ferry to Kaskaskia." Photograph by G. W. Eggleston, September 1891; courtesy of the Abraham Lincoln Presidential Library and Museum.

Fig. 6.15. "Kaskaskia Ferry Line. 'Bonny' and 'Jerry' Compound Grass
Burning Engines." Photograph by G. W. Eggleston, September 1891;
courtesy of the Abraham Lincoln Presidential Library and Museum.

Pierre Ménard established a simple, practical ferry across the Kaskaskia River in the early nineteenth century. The ferryman hauled the
ferry, large enough to carry a farm wagon, across the narrow river by
hand. Pierre Ménard's son Edmund continued to operate the ferry after
his father's death. There were relatively few bridges during the nineteenth
century, and those were mainly over creeks and small rivers. Ferries, such
as that at Kaskaskia, carried traffic across substantial rivers and competed with one another to provide service at the most convenient points.
When the Mississippi took over the channel of the Kaskaskia River, the
old hand-powered ferry was no longer practical, and it was replaced by
a larger, more powerful mule ferry, pictured in two photographs from
1891. Pacing mules turned a geared mechanism that moved the ferry
along a cable crossing the river (figs. 6.14, 6.15).

A ferry functioned near the site of old Kaskaskia as late as 1939. It finally
closed as construction began on the Chester Bridge, and the ferry operator,
officially the last inhabitant of old Kaskaskia, moved away. Six modern
ferries still cross the Mississippi where traffic does not warrant the expense
of bridges. The first bridge across the Mississippi was constructed at Min-
neapolis in 1854. Until 1942, when the Chester Bridge opened, there was
no bridge across the Mississippi between St. Louis and Cape Girardeau.

Fig. 6.16. Church at new Kaskaskia. Photograph by
MacDonald and Waters, summer 2015.

As the Mississippi drove the people from old Kaskaskia, people resettled
in nearby towns, some long established, such as Chester, others newly established. New Kaskaskia rose several miles to the southwest in the middle
of Kaskaskia Island, the name given to the land between the Mississippi's
waning old channel and the new channel taken from the Kaskaskia River.
There, the materials of the old brick church were used to build a new church
in a graceful early Gothic style (figs. 6.16–6.18). The church is now tech-
nically classified as a chapel, but services continue to be held on Saturday
afternoons. Although the church was badly damaged in the great flood of
1993, it has been beautifully restored, and it contains important relics of the
earlier churches, such as the carved wooden altar of 1736, eighteenth-century statues of Mary and Joseph, and an early chalice and paten.

The parishioners erected a new parochial residence beside the church,
and the Kaskaskia Bell State Memorial, a small brick building constructed

Fig. 6.17. Interior of the Church of the Immaculate Conception at new Kaskaskia. The hand-carved wooden altar and statuary have been part of the church since the eighteenth century. Photograph by Tina Fanetti; used with permission.

in 1948, stands beside the parochial residence. It houses the bell cast in 1741 and presented to the church by King Louis XV of France. The bell was rung on July 4, 1778, to announce the capture of Kaskaskia by George Rogers Clark and is known as the Liberty Bell of the West (fig. 6.19).

The bell bears an inscription of two lines. The upper line reads, "Pour l'eglise des Illinois par les soins du roi D'outreleau" (For the church of Illinois by courtesy of the king. D'outreleau). Father D'outreleau was the superior of the Society of Jesus, the Jesuits, in Illinois. The inscription has often been misread.[8] The lower line records the name of the bell caster, his location, and the date of manufacture, "I. B. M. Normand a la Rochelle 1741."

The old brick Kaskaskia Court House, subsequently employed as a school, was also rebuilt along its original lines, although with modern windows and doors (see fig. 4.7).

New Kaskaskia was a modest farming village, the population never more than a few hundred. Although far from the eroding riverbank, floods have repeatedly ravaged the town over the years, and with every major flood, the population declined. The great flood of 1993 was particularly devastating. The census of 2010 recorded just fourteen residents.

Fig. 6.18. Carved wooden altar, dating to 1736, in the Church of the Immaculate Conception at new Kaskaskia. Photograph by Tina Fanetti; used with permission.

The small town of Fort Gage emerged on the eastern side of the river close to the Ménard home, its name derived from the false impression that Fort Kaskaskia on the bluff above the town was Fort Gage. Fort Gage lasted until the automobile made a small town so close to Chester irrelevant.

The village of Riley's Mill prospered longer. The first mill on the site was built by Prisque Pagé about 1760 and abandoned after his death. General Edgar reestablished the mill about 1795. It served the people of Kaskaskia for years, but it eventually deteriorated and again closed. In 1832, Messrs. Feaman and Co. purchased the mill and put it back into service. In 1842, Feaman and Co. sold the mill to Daniel Reily and Sons. By 1855, the water mill was insufficient to meet demand. Reily added a steam-powered mill at the site, and he opened a general merchandise

Fig. 6.19. Kaskaskia's Liberty Bell of the West. Photograph
by MacDonald and Waters, summer 2015.

store (fig. 6.20). Daniel Reily died in 1867. He was buried in the Catholic
cemetery by the Church of the Conception, and his body was moved
along with many others in 1892 to the Garrison Hill Cemetery, where
his tombstone still stands (fig. 6.21).

A photo from the late nineteenth century shows two large mill buildings still nearly intact (fig. 6.22). A small town called Riley's Mill, disregard-
ing the spelling of Daniel Reily's name, developed below the mill at the base
of the hill and around the general store. Later it was called Riley's Lake,
for the pond that had powered the mill. At its height in the early twentieth
century, the town consisted of the mill, a grain elevator, stockyards, wood
and coal yard, several stores, a wagon maker's shop, post office, and ferry,
but it declined when the railroad built an embankment to elevate the
tracks through the middle of the town. The grain elevator closed in 1938.
The last manifestation of the town, the Riley Inn, survived some years
longer, but it too is gone now. The only remains visible today are a few
stone foundations and walls in the woods beside the road, visible in the
early spring but virtually hidden in foliage during the summer (fig. 6.23).

By 1913, the Mississippi had destroyed almost all traces of old Kaskaskia. The river now ran almost entirely in its new channel, and the old
channel was scarcely bigger than a creek. Today the upper part of the

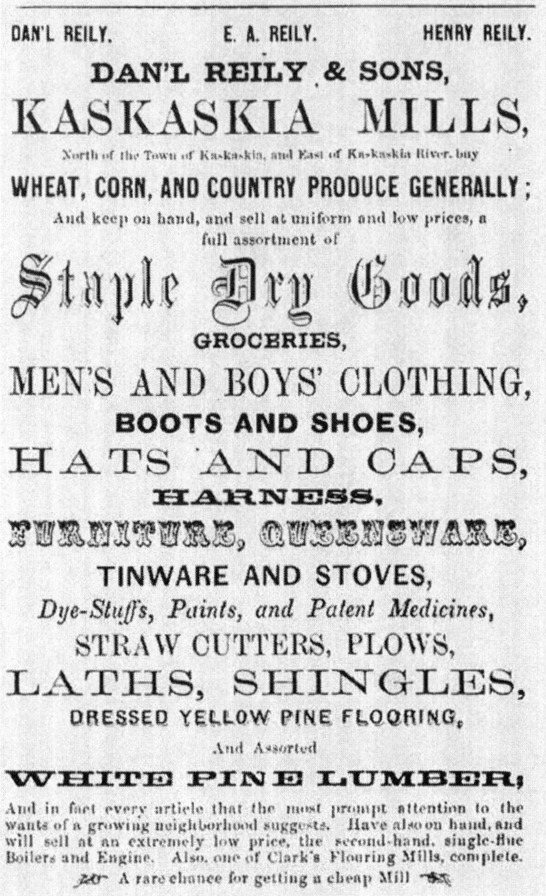

DAN'L REILY.   E. A. REILY.   HENRY REILY.

DAN'L REILY & SONS,

KASKASKIA MILLS,

North of the Town of Kaskaskia, and East of Kaskaskia River, buy

WHEAT, CORN, AND COUNTRY PRODUCE GENERALLY;

And keep on hand, and sell at uniform and low prices, a
full assortment of

Staple Dry Goods,

GROCERIES,

MEN'S AND BOYS' CLOTHING,

BOOTS AND SHOES,

HATS AND CAPS,

HARNESS,

FURNITURE, QUEENSWARE,

TINWARE AND STOVES,

Dye-Stuffs, Paints, and Patent Medicines,

STRAW CUTTERS, PLOWS,

LATHS, SHINGLES,

DRESSED YELLOW PINE FLOORING,

And Assorted

WHITE PINE LUMBER;

And in fact every article that the most prompt attention to the
wants of a growing neighborhood suggests. Have also on hand, and
will sell at an extremely low price, the second-hand, single-flue
Boilers and Engine. Also, one of Clark's Flouring Mills, complete.

☞ A rare chance for getting a cheap Mill ☜

Fig. 6.20. Reily store advertisement, 1859. E. J. Montague, *A Directory, Business Mirror, and Historical Sketches of Randolph County* (Alton: Courier Steam, 1859), 120.

old channel is generally an inconspicuous dry slough. The lower portion drains the water from the River aux Vases and Saline Creek into the Mississippi (figs. 6.24, 6.25).

In 1997, N. F. Norris conducted a survey, concluding that a small portion of the town site had not been completely consumed by the Mississippi and that some slight remnants may yet survive in the earth.[9] Norris reported that a foundation was then visible in the riverbank, and recently several gravestones from the Masonic cemetery have washed out of the bank. They, presumably, had been toppled and hidden by sediment during floods before the removal of graves in 1892 (fig. 6.26). The Mississippi continues to carry away the last surviving traces of the old town, but the river is ever changing. It also deposits silt, even on areas it recently cut away. Part of the area of old Kaskaskia is now in the channel of the Mississippi, and part lies under new land, Beaver Island, that the Mississippi has created.

Kaskaskia in its prime was much different from the village washed away by the river at the end of the nineteenth century. In the interval, Kaskaskia had been devastated and reduced by a series of disasters that

Fig. 6.21. Tombstone of Daniel Reily, 1809–1867, moved from the Catholic cemetery at Kaskaskia to the Garrison Hill Cemetery. Photograph by MacDonald and Waters, summer 2015.

Fig. 6.22. Mill buildings at Riley's Mill. From Elizabeth Holbrook, *Old 'Kaskia Days: A Novel* (Chicago: Schulte, 1893), between pp. 112 and 113.

Fig. 6.23. Stone building wall, at the site of the extinct town of Riley's Mill. Photograph by MacDonald and Waters, May 4, 2015.

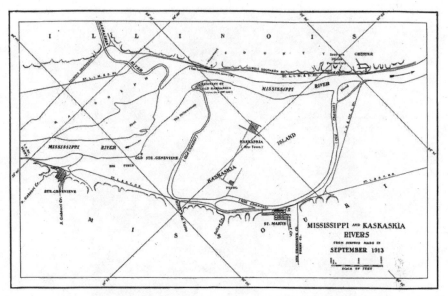

Fig. 6.24. Mississippi and Kaskaskia Rivers, 1913. From J. H. Burnham, "Destruction of Kaskaskia by the Mississippi River," *Transactions of the Illinois State Historical Society*, 1914, facing p. 105.

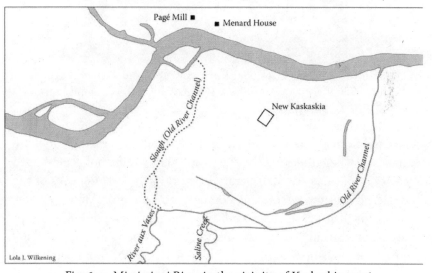

Fig. 6.25. Mississippi River in the vicinity of Kaskaskia, 2016.

Fig. 6.26. Masonic gravestone recently rescued from the bank of the
Mississippi River. Photograph by MacDonald and Waters, summer 2015.

gave credence to the notion of a curse. Kaskaskia, however, might have
recovered from all these calamities and even relocated earlier and more
extensively when threatened by the river had its vitality not been sapped
by a yet stronger force, demographic shift. In the first decades of the
nineteenth century, Americans flooded into Illinois and founded new
towns and villages across the state. The center of economic and political
power moved from the French-speaking population along the Mississippi to the English-speaking population in inland towns and emerging
cities. Kaskaskia began its long decline from the economic and political
center of Illinois to a quaint, historic town facing obliteration from the
remorseless river. Today all that survives is a small village a few miles
away from the original site but still bearing the name Kaskaskia and a
variety of artifacts, written documents, and photographs.

PART 2

DOMESTIC ARCHITECTURE
AT KASKASKIA

CHAPTER 7

INTRODUCTION

SKETCHES AND PHOTOGRAPHS of the lost homes of Kaskaskia show us the framework in which individuals lived their lives. The oldest Kaskaskia buildings of which we have a pictorial record were built in the decades of Kaskaskia's revival and prosperity, 1790–1820. Few eighteenth-century buildings of purely French colonial style survived at Kaskaskia far into the nineteenth century, none long enough to be photographed. The great floods of 1785 and 1844, the tornado of 1811, the earthquakes of 1811 and 1812, lesser floods, fires, and decay destroyed many buildings. Local prosperity during the early nineteenth century also led to the replacement of many early, apparently unpretentious buildings by larger and more substantial constructions. Most of the Kaskaskia buildings depicted in sketches or captured in photographs were either the chief public structures or the substantial homes of prominent members of the community. The homes of the humbler members of the community are poorly represented in surviving illustrations.

During the first decades of the nineteenth century, two architectural styles existed simultaneously at Kaskaskia, the Franco-American and Midwestern Federal styles, and later in the nineteenth century, a few buildings were renovated in Folk Victorian style. Buildings so modified or overlaid with additions are best described as eclectic.

FRANCO-AMERICAN STYLE

FRANCO-AMERICAN BUILDINGS WERE, as the name suggests, an amalgam of French and American elements. Earlier, purely French colonial buildings of the Illinois Country and Franco-American houses were both often constructed in the old French *poteaux en terre* or *poteaux sur sol* techniques. The outer walls of *poteaux en terre* buildings consisted of rot-resistant mulberry or cedar vertical posts positioned in trenches. The posts were then secured to top beams, and the area between the logs filled usually with *bousillage*, clay and grass, or *pierrotage*, clay and stone. Posts were typically left round belowground but hewed flat aboveground. The *poteaux sur sol* (posts on sill) technique was similar, but the vertical posts were secured at the bottom to a sill that sat on a foundation. Such buildings were often covered with clapboard siding in the nineteenth century, which makes it difficult or impossible to discern the construction technique from a photograph or sketch. French colonial and Franco-American buildings in Illinois were also sometimes constructed of stone. An excellent example is the Franco-American home of Jean-Baptiste Ducoigne, built about 1803. Both French colonial and Franco-American houses were generally single-story buildings, although attic areas were used for living space or storage.

There were also easily recognizable differences between the French colonial and Franco-American styles. Purely French buildings seldom incorporated attic dormers, while Franco-American houses often included dormers to provide light in the attics, and dormers were often added later to early French houses. Early French colonial houses in the Illinois Country were initially built without a *gallerie* (porch), but during the late eighteenth century, the style often incorporated galleries on one, two, three, or four sides. Franco-American homes at Kaskaskia usually had just one gallerie on the front.

The roof construction of the two styles differed as well. French colonial roofs were usually double-pitched and steeply angled over the walled portion of the structure and were shallower over the galleries. Franco-American buildings typically had single-pitch rooflines extending from the peak to the edge of the gallerie. Purely French colonial buildings were usually hip-roofed. Some French colonial constructions did incorporate vertical gable-end roofs, but such roofs were rare in the Illinois Country until the early nineteenth century, when they became characteristic of the Franco-American style. When extensive renovations were required, the roofs of French colonial houses were often rebuilt in the Franco-American style. In addition to photographs and sketches of the lost Franco-American-style house of Kaskaskia, Franco-American buildings are represented by surviving examples in Ste. Geneviève and Prairie du Rocher (figs. 7.1, 7.2) and once existed in St. Louis.

Fig. 7.1. French colonial style: Bequet-Ribault House, Ste. Geneviève. Photograph by MacDonald and Waters, spring 2015.

Fig. 7.2. Franco-American style: the Creole House, Prairie du Rocher. The original single-room structure was built about 1800 and expanded laterally several times into the 1830s. Photograph by MacDonald and Waters, autumn 2015.

Fig. 7.3. Midwestern Federal style: Colonel Benjamin Stephenson House, built in 1820, Edwardsville, Illinois. Ornamentation is here much reduced, but characteristic symmetry and proportions are maintained. Photograph by MacDonald and Waters, spring 2016.

MIDWESTERN FEDERAL STYLE

GEORGIAN-STYLE ARCHITECTURE, CHARACTERIZED by symmetry, classical proportions, and subdued ornamentation, was popular in Britain throughout much of the eighteenth century and first decades of the nineteenth century. Architectural pattern books brought the style to New England, where local adaptation preserved the essential characteristics of the British originals in a generally simplified form. New England colonial Georgian homes were usually rectangular and symmetrical with a paneled front door at the center. The front door was regularly ornamented with flanking flattened columns and a decorative crown over the door. The standard design featured four windows on the ground floor arranged symmetrically, two on each side of the door, and five windows across the front of the second floor. The houses often had symmetrically paired chimneys, and roofs were single-pitched with minimal roof overhang and no porch. The New England colonial Georgian style seamlessly evolved into the American Federal style. Federal-style buildings continued the basic forms of the colonial Georgian, but they were even less elaborate.

Characteristically, the Federal style continued to emphasize symmetry and classical proportions, but decorative items, such as attached flattened columns and moldings, were narrower and simpler than in the colonial Georgian style. Americans migrating to Illinois after the American Revolution brought the Federal style to Kaskaskia, where it underwent more modifications. Midwestern Federal houses were generally even simpler than New England Federal houses, with decorative stylings often omitted entirely or reduced to a bare minimum. The largest houses most closely conformed to the standard New England Federal style, while the small homes were often more flexible in design. Homes with only one chimney, often centrally located, were common. Some were slightly asymmetrical, allowing larger rooms on one side. Others completely disregarded the symmetry that characterized the standard Federal style by incorporating multiple entrances and, in the most radical instances, even utilizing gable ends as secondary "fronts." The Midwestern Federal style could be found in many contemporaneous communities in the Northwest Territory (fig. 7.3).

FOLK VICTORIAN AND ECLECTIC HOUSES

LITTLE WAS BUILT in Kaskaskia in the last half of the nineteenth century, but remodeling introduced elements of Folk Victorian style into the community. Although not as elaborate as the urban Victorian mansions of the rich, Folk Victorian houses exhibited the same stylistic elements: lathe-turned spindles used as porch posts, decorative brackets under the eaves, and ornamental trim (fig. 7.4). The power lathe and the power jigsaw, innovations of the early industrial age, made these elements readily available and affordable. Such decorative elements could be ordered from catalogues and delivered by riverboat or freight train.

Builders of Folk Victorian houses often favored an L-shaped ground plan, a wing attached at a right angle to the main block of the house. In the mid-nineteenth century, similar rear wings were often added to existing rectangular Midwestern Federal houses, producing the fashionable L-shape configuration. Some late Midwestern Federal houses, such as the Kaskaskia parochial residence, were initially constructed with a rear wing.

Other houses were so modified over time with ad hoc additions that their original character was largely lost, and they emerged as eclectic buildings defying simple classification.

Fig. 7.4. Folk Victorian style: a house in Galena, Illinois.
Photograph courtesy of David E. Taylor, © 1997.

CHAPTER 8

FRANCO-AMERICAN HOMES
OF KASKASKIA

THE PIERRE MÉNARD HOUSE

PIERRE MÉNARD WAS one of the most distinguished citizens of Kaskaskia and all of Illinois, and his home on the bluff across the river from the village was the grandest home in the area (fig. 8.1). Recent research reveals that the building was built in stages. On the main level the three large central rooms were constructed about 1802. The three smaller rooms to the rear were constructed next, and the two rooms at the back corners

Fig. 8.1. Pierre Ménard House. Photograph by
MacDonald and Waters, spring 2015.

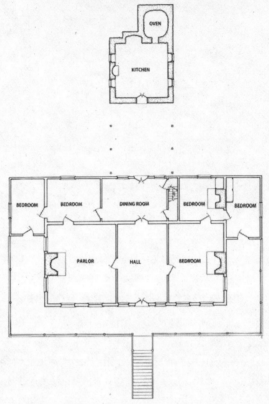

Fig. 8.2. Plan of the main floor of the Pierre Ménard House.
Derived from the American Historic Buildings Survey plan. http://
www.loc.gov/pictures/collection/hh/item/il0219.sheet.00001a/.

last, about 1818 (fig. 8.2).[1] The room at the back right corner was used
by Pierre Ménard as his business office. Behind the main structure was
a separate kitchen, now connected to the main house by a shared roof.

The front view forcefully recalls the French plantation homes of the
southern Mississippi Valley and Louisiana, single-story buildings on
raised foundations to protect them from ground moisture and flooding.
Apart from this semblance, however, the Ménard home is much different. It is located on the lower portion of a bluff, above the flood level.
The front pillars simply provide a level foundation for the gallerie on
the uneven, sloping ground, and behind the front foundation pillars are
stone-built storage rooms. The architecturally sophisticated, complex
roof is explained by J. R. Luer and J. W. Francis: "The hipped roof has the
ridge being off-center and closer to the rear wall. This placement of the

ridge makes the front hip much larger on the front and each end and a pair of matching chimneys gives the illusion that the house is larger than it is. In 1812 the roof was changed and the very Anglo looking dormers were added to light two additional bedrooms."[2]

The Pierre Ménard House is a state historic site, generally open for guided tours from May through October. It is richly furnished with some of the original Ménard family possessions and other contemporary pieces, such as a sideboard from the home of Shadrach Bond, Illinois's first governor. Ménard's office is particularly interesting, looking as if he had just stepped out for a moment. The basement contains a small but excellent museum, which includes many original pieces such as one of Pierre Ménard's original Indian agent account books and a dinner bell presented to Ménard by Shadrach Bond.

The exterior of the Ménard home is in need of maintenance. Illinois is in financial crisis at the time of writing, but one can only hope that shortsighted budgetary concerns will not damage this architectural gem and tourist attraction that has, with justification, been called the "Monticello of the West."

Pierre Ménard was born on October 7, 1766, at St. Antoine-sur-Richelieu in Canada, near Montréal (fig. 8.3).[3] He came to Vincennes about 1786. Colonel Joseph Maria Francesco Vigo, more commonly known as François Vigo, employed the young Ménard and provided him with valuable experience in business dealings with Indians, Creole French, and Americans. Through Vigo, Ménard met and established relations with important business and political figures. For example, in 1789, Vigo and Ménard traveled to Carlisle, Pennsylvania, where they met with George Washington to discuss the situation in the West.

About 1790, Ménard and a partner opened a store in Kaskaskia. Ménard soon bought out his partner and went on to become a leading merchant and Indian trader. Until his death in 1844, over half a century later, he competed against or joined in ventures with virtually all the other contemporary early fur traders and great merchants in the central Mississippi Valley, including the Vallés, the Chouteaus, Manuel Lisa, William Morrison, and Hugh Maxwell. In 1809, Ménard, a partner in the Missouri Fur Company of St. Louis, accompanied two other partners, Jean-Pierre Chouteau and Manuel Lisa, and a large contingent of men on a trapping and trading expedition up the Missouri River as far north as the Three Forks of the Missouri. The expedition did not end

Fig. 8.3. Portrait of Pierre Ménard, engraving after a painting,
in the Chicago History Museum, formerly attributed to Chester
Harding. Edward G. Mason, *Early Chicago and Illinois*, vol. 4 of *Chicago
Historical Society's Collections* (Chicago: Fergus, 1890), 142.

well. The Blackfeet Indians were hostile and killed eight members of
the expedition, including several of Ménard's friends. The expedition
retreated, and Ménard never again aspired to be a mountain man,[4] but
rather he stayed in Kaskaskia and promoted his trade connections there.

In addition to his mercantile interests, Ménard held many military and
public offices. In 1795, Governor St. Clair appointed Ménard a major in the
Randolph County militia. He held that rank until 1806, when Governor
William Henry Harrison promoted him to lieutenant colonel and ranking
officer of the First Regiment of Randolph County militia. For a decade,
between 1801 and 1811, Pierre Ménard was judge of the county court of
common pleas, and for much of that time, 1802 to 1809, he was simultaneously an associate judge of the territorial supreme court. From 1803
to 1809, Ménard served in the legislature of the Indiana Territory, which
included Illinois at that time. When Illinois became a separate territory in

1809, Ménard resigned his judgeship in the Indiana Territory. The Illinois territorial legislature, consisting of a council and a house of representatives, was first constituted in 1812. Pierre Ménard served as the presiding officer of the council from 1812 until 1818, when Illinois became a state.

As Illinois moved toward statehood, Ménard was one of the group selected to write the constitution. When Illinois achieved statehood in 1818, Ménard was a nearly unanimous choice for lieutenant governor. He had, however, only become a US citizen officially in 1816, far short of the Illinois constitutional requirement that the lieutenant governor be a US citizen for at least thirty years prior to election. The legislature held Ménard in such high regard that it quickly reduced the requirement to two years, and he was duly elected. Ménard served as lieutenant governor until 1822. Throughout his public service, Ménard avoided aligning himself with any faction and strived for moderation and consensus.

In 1813, Ménard became the regional subagent for Indian affairs, a post he held until 1833, when the last Illinois Indians were removed from the state. Indian agents provided supplies to tribes according to treaty agreements and charged the US government accordingly. Many agents were notoriously corrupt, providing the Indians with substandard and inadequate supplies and overcharging the government. No such suspicions were ever attached to Pierre Ménard, who was held in high regard by the Indians, both in his role as government agent and as Indian trader. A story, told in many minor variants, claims that when a group of Indians had come to Kaskaskia to trade their furs to Ménard, an Anglo-American trader asked why they did not trade with him. The Indians replied that they would rather trade their furs to Pierre Ménard at half their worth than receive twice their value from any of the "Long Knives."

In 1824, a delegation of Cherokee and Shawnee chiefs paused at Ménard's home while traveling to meet with President James Monroe. There, Takatoka, the Cherokee spokesman for the delegation, suddenly died. The delegation asked Ménard to take his place, and together with the Cherokee and Shawnee chiefs, he traveled to Washington, where he ably represented the Indians' concerns to the president. In 1828, President John Quincy Adams appointed Pierre Ménard and Lewis Cass of Michigan "Commissioners of the United States, with full power and authority to hold conference and to conclude and sign a treaty or treaties with the Chippewas, Ottawas, Pattawattimas, Winnebagoes, Fox and Sacs Nations of Indians."[5] They succeeded, ending hostilities in northern

Fig. 8.4. Ménard monument, dedicated in 1888, on the grounds of the state capitol in Springfield. Charles Chouteau, donor; J. H. Mahoney, sculptor. Photograph by L. Senalik; used with permission.

Illinois and southern Wisconsin. On a number of occasions, Ménard sent supplies at his personal expense to Indians tribes in distress, and he attempted to use his position as Indian subagent to protect Indians from white aggression. When the last of the Illinois Indians left the state in 1833, Ménard hired a steamboat to carry them west.

Ménard, like almost all prosperous men of his age and area, was a slave owner. He seems to have been paternalistic and humane toward his slaves, but, of course, slavery remained inherently oppressive.

Throughout his career, Ménard was noted for his hospitality and generosity. He was sensitive to others' self-esteem, so often rather than dispensing charity, he made small loans to people in need. His papers, examined after his death, included a great number of notes for such loans that he had never attempted to collect. His charitable contributions and those of his wife were made without display or publicity. He supported the sisters of the Order of the Visitation with gifts and loans on extremely favorable terms, enabling them to build their convent and academy, which they named after him.

Pierre Ménard died shortly before his seventy-eighth birthday, as the rising waters of the great flood of 1844 were about to engulf Kaskaskia. The parish registry records, as his body was conveyed to the church for burial, "thither he was accompanied by an immense concourse of People."[6] The prominent jurist John Dean Caton, justice of the Illinois Supreme Court and a native of Kaskaskia, reminisced that "Pierre Menard was the best man I ever knew."[7] A statue of Pierre Ménard stands on the grounds of the state capitol in Springfield, the funds for which were donated by the Chouteau family, a testament to the enduring respect for Pierre Ménard (fig. 8.4).[8]

THE NATHANIEL POPE HOUSE

THE CURRIE SKETCH of the Nathaniel Pope House reveals a Franco-American-style home with some atypical features (fig. 8.5). Exceptionally, the front gallerie is lined by a guardrail and entered from the end rather than at the middle. The door to the home is at the opposite end of the gallerie from the entrance to the gallerie. Perhaps this arrangement was made to provide a play area for the Pope children.

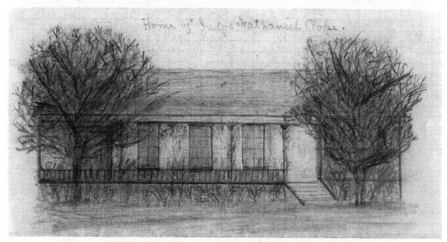

Fig. 8.5. Sketch of the Nathaniel Pope House by Mrs. H. S. Currie, circa 1865. Inscribed "Home of Judge Nathaniel Pope." Courtesy of the Abraham Lincoln Presidential Library and Museum.

Nathaniel Pope was born in Kentucky in 1784. He practiced law at Ste. Geneviève from 1804 until 1808, when he moved to Kaskaskia in anticipation of Congress organizing the Illinois Territory. Pope had influential connections in Washington, DC; his brother was a senator from Kentucky. In 1809, President James Madison appointed Pope's cousin, Ninian Edwards, the territorial governor and Pope the territorial secretary, a post he held until 1816, when he was elected territorial delegate to the US Congress. Nathaniel Pope and his nephew Daniel Pope Clark played important roles in the admission of Illinois to statehood, and they were principally responsible for depriving Wisconsin of a large section of land that was added to Illinois's northern border. That territory today comprises Illinois's thirteen northern counties and includes the city of Chicago.

In 1819, President James Monroe appointed Nathaniel Pope to the newly formed US District Court for Illinois, a post he held for the rest of his life. Pope continued to reside in Kaskaskia until 1844. In the aftermath of the great flood of that year, he moved to Alton, where he died in 1850.

ODILE MÉNARD MAXWELL HOUSE

THE HOUSE WHERE Pierre Ménard's eldest daughter and her husband lived was built in 1808.[9] It consisted of a single story on a stone foundation with a front gallerie (fig. 8.6). The gable end of the house, visible in the sketch, is covered with clapboards, while the front of the home beneath the gallerie appears smooth and white. The house, like many other early Kaskaskia houses, was probably of *poteaux sur sol* construction. The roofline is distinctly American—a single slope from a peak, with flat gables—and does not have the profile of an earlier French hip roof.

Marie Odile Ménard was born in 1793, the eldest daughter of Pierre Ménard and one of thirteen children. In 1811, she married Hugh Charles Maxwell. An immigrant from Ireland, he was a nephew of Father James Maxwell, the controversial and worldly priest and vicar general of Upper Louisiana, who presided at Ste. Geneviève. The couple had eleven children.

Hugh Maxwell ran a successful store in Kaskaskia, at first in partnership with William Shannon and then as sole proprietor (fig. 8.7).[10] He was a competitor and sometimes collaborator with William Morrison and Pierre Ménard, both of whom also owned stores. Much more than

Fig. 8.6. Sketch of the home of Odile Ménard Maxwell by Mrs. H. S. Currie, circa 1865. Inscribed "Home Of Madame Odeli [*sic*] Menard Maxwell." Courtesy of the Abraham Lincoln Presidential Library and Museum.

country general stores, they were wholesale centers, importing bulk material from the East and from New Orleans and selling to lesser stores in smaller communities. There was little money in circulation, and most business was conducted by barter, with stores accepting and exporting local farm produce and furs and hides from hunters, trappers, and Indians coming from the West.

CHEAP NEW GOODS.

HUGH H. MAXWELL & CO. are now opening at the said Maxwell's New House, in Kaskaskia, a very GENERAL ASSORTMENT OF *MERCHANDIZE*, Lately imported from Philadelphia and Baltimore, which they can afford to sell, and will sell upon the most moderate terms. Jan. 1, 1818.

Fig. 8.7. Hugh Maxwell's advertisement from the *Western Intelligencer*, January 6, 1818.

The reference in the newspaper notice to "Maxwell's New Home at Kaskaskia" probably refers to the Midwestern Federal home later inhabited by Hugh Maxwell's eldest son, Ferdinand, rather than the older home where his mother continued to live. The store was on a lot adjoining the "new home."

Hugh died of cholera on September 4, 1833, during an epidemic.[11] By that time, Kaskaskia's trade had declined greatly, and Hugh left his wife and children in reduced circumstances. Ferdinand took over the management of the family store, and the Ménard family aided Odile.

Lucien Bonaparte Maxwell, the second son of Hugh and Odile, went west with John C. Frémont and Kit Carson to California. In 1844, at Taos, New Mexico, Lucien married Luz Beaubien, daughter of Carlos Beaubien, who, with his partner Guadalupe Miranda, held a land grant of a million acres. Through inheritance and purchase Lucien acquired much of the land grant and additional parcels of land, a holding eventually totaling more than 1.7 million acres. Lucien financed his land purchases and colorful lifestyle largely though selling supplies to the US Army and to trappers and miners, many of whom mined gold on land leased from Lucien.[12] Ferdinand Maxwell, whose house was also sketched by Mrs. H. S. Currie, followed his younger brother Lucien to New Mexico in 1859.

In 1859, E. J. Montague wrote that Odile Ménard Maxwell

> is yet living in Kaskaskia. She has spent her whole life in the village of her nativity, and has occupied the house where she now resides for more than forty years. She has in her possession a Damask rose bush, which was brought from New Orleans more than a century ago. It is the first rose bush that ever bloomed in Illinois, and though it has been swept over by the floods of the last hundred years, it still retains its vigor and bloom, putting forth its sprouts upon the annual recurrence of springtime.[13]

THE DUCOIGNE HOUSE

THE DUCOIGNES RESIDED in a handsome Franco-American house. Jean-Baptiste Ducoigne and then his son Louis-Jefferson Ducoigne, both paramount chiefs of the Kaskaskia Indians, lived in the house. It was constructed in accordance with the second Treaty of Vincennes, August 13, 1803, which contained a provision that the government would have a

Fig. 8.8. Ducoigne House. Photograph by Max von Fragstein, Chester, Illinois, 1893. Courtesy of the Abraham Lincoln Presidential Library and Museum.

house built for Jean-Baptiste at Kaskaskia and enclose one hundred acres for him. The house stood to the east of the convent in the countryside, a short distance from the village of Kaskaskia. It was built of stone and appears, in figure 8.8, neatly whitewashed. The vertical gable ends and a single-slope roof, from its peak to the edge of a gallerie, are markedly American characteristics imposed on what is basically a French form.

Jean-Baptiste Ducoigne became the paramount chief of the Kaskaskia in 1774 and held that position until his death in 1811. He was one of the most fascinating people to have lived in Kaskaskia and one of the least appreciated today. Louis-Jefferson Ducoigne succeeded his father as paramount chief and lived in the house until his death, sometime between 1824 and 1832. Later, Raphael Widen, a justice of the peace and clerk for the firm of Ménard and Vallé, lived in the house.[14]

"UNCLE JACK" BACKUS HOUSE

A SKETCH BY Mrs. H. S. Currie (fig. 8.9) provides a rare example of a simple cabin in the Franco-American style that can be attributed to a specific individual, the free African American "Uncle Jack" Backus.[15] The building is a one- or two-room cabin with no indication of clapboards or other siding. Although the lower portion of the building is largely obscured, the cabin seems to have been built on a limestone foundation, probably constructed by the *poteaux sur sol* technique. The cabin was whitewashed, giving it a neat and uniform appearance. The fireplace and chimney were built of local limestone, abundant on the bluffs on the eastern side of the Kaskaskia River. The cabin has no gallerie. The roof appears to have been covered with long wooden planks, one of several types of roofing of humbler dwellings in the Illinois Country.

Mrs. Currie's inscription, though paternalistic and racist, evidences real affection for the elderly African American called "Uncle Jack" Backus, who had been a servant in the home of Judge Nathaniel Pope.[16] Jack Backus is listed in the 1825 state census for Kaskaskia as a "Free Negro." The US Census of 1860 lists a John Backus, an African American living in Kaskaskia, estimated to be ninety years old and originally from Virginia.[17] These two census records almost certainly refer to same man, as Jack was a common nickname for John. In 1860, John Backus was living in a household with Peter Backus, twenty-two, and Lyatt Backus, twenty-five. Both John and Peter are listed as farmers.

We know nothing certain about Jack Backus's early life, but his origin in Virginia, his age, and his free status indicate that he may have been a beneficiary of one of the greatest acts of conscience in Illinois history. Edward Coles was born in 1786 into one of the first families of Virginia, the plantation and slave-owning elite. He grew up as part of the social circle that included Jefferson, Madison, Monroe, the Randolphs, and other slave owners of wealth and prominence, but Coles's education led him to the realization that Enlightenment ideals were incompatible with slavery.

After serving as President Madison's personal secretary, during which time he undertook a diplomatic mission to Russia, Coles sold his lands in Virginia and purchased land in the American Bottom in Illinois. In 1819, he loaded his goods and seventeen slaves on two boats and traveled down the Ohio River to Illinois. On the river he announced the emancipation of his slaves and told them they were absolutely free to go ashore or to continue accompanying him. In Illinois, Coles provided each individual with a certificate of emancipation, gave freeholds of 160 acres to the heads of families who wished to farm, and continued to employ and aid others. All of this considerably reduced Coles's wealth.

Fig. 8.9. Sketch of the home of "Uncle Jack" Backus by Mrs. H. S. Currie, circa 1865. The inscription reads "Home of Uncle Jack Backus. The favorite servant of the Pope's. The old darkey never seemed so happy as when recalling the memories of the family history. It was with greatest pride he would predict his Young Master John Pope would be a Genl.— if we ever had a war.— His Young Master William being so handsome he captured the heart of the lovely granddaughter of Genl. Russell of St. Louis. His beautiful twin Mistresses Miss Lucretia and Miss Cynthia so alike tho one a blonde and the other a brunette were frequently called the 'Pope Angels' as they many times accompanied their distinguished father to the bench of the Supreme Court— that he had always ended his story by saying Miss Penelopie [*sic*] was his favorite." Courtesy of the Abraham Lincoln Presidential Library and Museum.

President Madison appointed Coles registrar of the land office at Edwardsville, Illinois, where Coles quickly earned a reputation for honesty and intelligence. This led to his election as governor of the state in late 1822. As governor he resolutely opposed attempts to establish slavery in the state and urged the abolition of slavery in disguised forms, such as ninety-nine-year indentures. John Backus may have been one of the slaves Edward Coles freed, perhaps a household servant subsequently employed by Nathaniel Pope, who worked alongside Coles in the land office of Edwardsville.

ANONYMOUS CABIN

MOST PICTORIAL REPRESENTATIONS of Kaskaskia homes can be connected to specific individuals, almost always to a member of the town's elite. Houses of the less prominent members of the community seldom attracted the notice of those who photographed buildings during Kaskaskia's last days. An image of an anonymous cabin offers a rare glimpse of an ordinary dwelling (figs. 8.10, 8.11).

The side of the cabin facing the observer is covered with clapboard, disguising the basic nature of the construction, but the front of the house under the gallerie reveals the old French *poteaux sur sol* construction

Fig. 8.10. Vertical-log cabin. Photograph probably by J. G. Miller, May 8, 1900. Courtesy of the Abraham Lincoln Presidential Library and Museum.

Fig. 8.11. Street scene in Kaskaskia. Photograph by J. G. Miller, May 8, 1900. The vertical-log cabin appears at the extreme left of the photograph. In the background at the far left is the courthouse and at the right, the parochial residence. Courtesy of the Abraham Lincoln Presidential Library and Museum.

technique. Whitewash would normally have covered the entire wall, but here it is worn, exposing the timbers to view. In early houses built by the wealthy, the timbers employed were of substantial size. Houses of the less affluent and houses constructed later, when timber was less readily available, often employed smaller timbers, as was the case here.

The roof of the cabin is distinctly different from the common French colonial double-pitched hip roof. Here the roof is single-pitched, forming an unbroken line from its peak to the bottom edge of the gallerie, terminating laterally in a vertical gable end. At the back of the house is an *appentis*, a lean-to added considerably later than the initial construction. The roofline of this appentis is slightly different from that of the main building, and the appentis is constructed from milled boards in the later frame technique.

Internally, the house was almost certainly divided into just two rooms. The main room occupied the entire side of the house left of the front door and was served by the major fireplace. This arrangement of rooms was common in small cabins and even larger eighteenth-century French dwellings. A second, smaller chimney is visible, slightly offset toward the rear, on the far side of the house and was probably a late addition.

The main fireplace was constructed of local limestone and the chimney of brick. This technique was common at Kaskaskia. Limestone was preferred for fireplaces because it was readily available for free and was more resistant to heat than the locally available brick, but a brick chimney could be made thinner and lighter than limestone, always a consideration for the soft soil of Kaskaskia. The first brick kilns were constructed at Kaskaskia in the mid-1830s to provide material for the convent, and only subsequently did brick become common building material at Kaskaskia. Brick buildings were constructed locally before that date, but the bricks had to be brought in by boat from a great distance at a significant cost. If the partial brick chimney was part of the original construction, the anonymous cabin was probably constructed between about 1840 and 1860, an exceptionally late survivor of the French vertical-log construction technique. More likely, the roof and chimney were Americanized modifications of a much earlier French *poteaux sur sol* cabin, as is commonly seen in extant houses of much grander design in Ste. Geneviève. The original building may have lost its roof to decay or perhaps a storm, such as the tornado that stuck Kaskaskia in 1811.

Figure 8.11 provides the location of the cabin in relation to two buildings, the parochial residence and the Kaskaskia Court House, whose locations are well known. (See the map of Kaskaskia in figure 5.12.) This is one of the few photographs to include some of the last inhabitants of old Kaskaskia.

CHAPTER 9

MIDWESTERN FEDERAL
AND ECLECTIC HOUSES
AND THEIR OWNERS

SHADRACH BOND HOUSE

G. W. SMITH, a nineteenth- and early twentieth-century historian of
southern Illinois, wrote that Shadrach Bond called his farm in the countryside near Kaskaskia "Elvirade."[1] There he built a substantial home of
bricks brought from Pittsburgh on flatboats. The style is traditionally
Federal, with five windows across the second story, four windows and a
centrally located door (with a modest transom window above it) on the
first story, and symmetrically arranged chimneys (fig. 9.1). The house
departs from the Federal model only by the addition of a single-story
attachment, which on occasion Bond made available to businessmen
newly established in Kaskaskia.

Shadrach Bond (1773–1832; fig. 9.2[2]) was born in Maryland and im-
migrated to Illinois in 1794, following the lead of his namesake uncle
with whom he is sometimes confused. Bond settled briefly in the town
of New Design and then moved to Kaskaskia. He prospered in Illinois,
acquiring a substantial farm and actively speculating in land. For several
terms, he served as a member of the General Assembly of the Indiana
Territory, which then included Illinois. From late 1812 until the autumn
of 1814, he was the territorial delegate to the US Congress. He subsequently became the receiver of public monies at Kaskaskia and one of
the partners in the City and Bank Company of Cairo, which collapsed

Fig. 9.1. Shadrach Bond House. John Corson Smith, *History of Freemasonry in Illinois* (Chicago: Rogers and Smith, 1905), between pp. 32 and 33.

Fig. 9.2. Portrait of Shadrach Bond, engraving after an oil painting made during Bond's lifetime. *Portrait and Biographical Record of Randolph, Jackson, Perry and Monroe Counties, Illinois* (Chicago: Biographical Publishing, 1894), 110.

when the chief partner died suddenly before the town or bank could be established.

In 1818, Shadrach Bond was elected, without opposition, the first governor of the newly established state of Illinois. In 1823, Bond became the registrar of the land office at Kaskaskia, and in the next year he ran for Congress but lost. In 1827, he served on a board of commissioners to locate a site for the state penitentiary. He died in 1832.

Bond was buried on his farm, but by 1879 the encroaching Mississippi approached the grave site, and Bond's remains were moved to Evergreen Cemetery in Chester.[3] By 1892, the Mississippi threatened Bond's by-then-abandoned home. William H. Doza purchased the house and demolished it, salvaging the bricks and other materials from which he built a charming house in Dozaville, although in a much different style from that of the Bond home.

WILLIAM MORRISON /
COL. WILLIAM THOMPSON HOUSE

MRS. CURRIE MADE two sketches of the same building. The sketch now at the Abraham Lincoln Presidential Library differs from the one at the University of Illinois Library (fig. 9.3) by the addition of two trees by the sides of the house and the substitution of the words "Col. Wm. Thomson" for "Col. Morrison" in the inscription. We have not succeeded in identifying Colonel William Thomson. Could Mrs. Currie, who sketched the house about thirty years after Morrison's death, have simply confused the names Thomson and Morrison?

The house was built in 1801 and stood on Elm Street at the corner of Poplar.[4] It was an early and excellent example of Midwestern Federal. The arrangement of four windows on the first floor, five on the second, and two chimneys symmetrically located toward the ends of the house is true Federal style, and only the lack of ornamentation around the door marks the building as Midwestern Federal. Exceptionally, it was built of stone. It was here that William Morrison gave a ball for Lafayette in 1825, attended by all the notables of Kaskaskia and the governor of Illinois.

Sister Mary Josephine Barber, one of the sisters from the Order of the Visitation who traveled to Kaskaskia in 1833 to found the first convent in Illinois and a school for young ladies, wrote a description

Fig. 9.3. Sketch of the Col. Morrison House by Mrs. H. S. Currie, circa 1865. Inscribed "Residence of Col. Morrison where La Fayette [*sic*] was entertained. In 1862, the place was sold to a Mr. Dennis Kavanaugh who used the stone in building a home for his family on a farm about two miles from the Bond Place." Original in MS 575, Illinois History and Lincoln Collections, University Library, University of Illinois at Urbana-Champaign.

of the home of William Morrison. Sister Barber, from a sophisticated background, found Kaskaskia in the 1830s unimpressive, except for Morrison's home:

> Far from suspecting that we were in the midst of the town, we were still on the lookout for it, when our carriages stopped in front of Mr. Wm. Morrison's elegant stone mansion, the only real building in the place. . . . Alighting at Mr. Wm. Morrison's, his wife and sister-in-law received us most graciously. . . . Theirs was a double house and very roomy, though only two stories and an attic. The entire second story was appropriated to our use. We had one small and two large bed-rooms, besides the ball-room, which ran the entire width of the house, over the parlors; but no one slept in this, nor was it any longer used for its original purpose, it being deemed unsafe on account of a fissure in the wall caused by the earthquake[s] of 18[11–1812]; since which time Kaskaskia, having rapidly depopulated, had little call for large ball-rooms or brilliant assemblies. The sisters used to walk there to recite their office, etc.[5]

On the first evening of our arrival, we remarked that the parlor floors were not perfectly level, but wavy. Madam William informed us that this as well as the rent in the east wall had been occasioned by the earthquake.[6]

As Mrs. H. S. Currie noted on her sketch, the William Morrison House was demolished for its materials in 1862.

William Morrison (1763–1837) was one of the most famous early residents of Illinois and Kaskaskia.[7] In 1790, Guy Bryan of Philadelphia formed a trading company with his nephew William Morrison, who went west and settled in Kaskaskia. When Morrison arrived, the Illinois fur trade moved along traditional lines to Canada, either through Michillimackinac or directly to Montréal, and merchants sent agricultural products, lead, and deer hides south to New Orleans. Bryan and Morrison intended to change the direction of trade, sending goods from Philadelphia by wagon to Pittsburgh and then down the Ohio River to Illinois or, alternatively, from Philadelphia to New Orleans by ship and from there up the Mississippi to Illinois; returning trade goods from Illinois retraced those same routes. The partners grew wealthy.

Morrison sometimes cooperated with other merchants at Kaskaskia, Ste. Geneviève, and St. Louis for their mutual benefit and sometimes competed vigorously against them. He opened branch stores in several communities, had goods carted to the lead district of Missouri to sell to the miners, and entered into contracts with the government to deliver the mail and to provide rations for military posts and supplies to friendly Indian tribes according to treaty agreements. Morrison even became directly engaged in the Indian trade, sending out employees with goods to trade directly with relatively nearby tribes, investing with individual traders who ventured further afield, and entering into a short-lived partnership to trade on the distant upper Missouri River. General merchandising and government contracts, particularly during the War of 1812, brought Morrison the most profits.

There was little cash circulating in Illinois, and most local business was done by barter. All manner of goods were accepted in payment, but the most important means of exchange was furs, which were loaded on supply boats returning up the Ohio River to Pittsburgh and then overland to Philadelphia. Boats returning to New Orleans were loaded with products such as flour, salt, lead, and deer skins, and they were either sold in New Orleans or carried by ship to Philadelphia or other eastern markets.

The ledger of William Morrison's Kaskaskia store for the years from 1805 to 1831 is preserved in the Chester Public Library, which, with the aid of a digitization grant from the Illinois State Library, has made the ledger available online. This fascinating document of 655 pages lists over 1,200 customers, local citizens, settlers coming to Illinois and Missouri, boatmen, Indians, and Indian traders.[8]

While Morrison made great profits during the War of 1812, his business was beginning to decline by 1815. Bryan retired, ending their partnership. Morrison's aggressive business practices alienated important French Creole merchants and traders in St. Louis just as St. Louis was becoming the economic hub of the region and center of the Indian trade. New towns and roads, and the growth of steamboat traffic, also brought competition to Morrison's enterprises. The Panic of 1819 and subsequent economic shifts disrupted business, and by 1820 Morrison was in some economic distress. By 1822, even his Kaskaskia store was much reduced in sales, although he kept it open until shortly before his death in 1837.

Many of the important traders and merchants were deeply involved in government, holding a variety of offices over the course of years. Morrison was an exception, holding only a couple of minor judicial offices and local posts and then not for long. He seems not to have been interested in this sort of service, and undoubtedly his many and varied mercantile endeavors demanded virtually all of his time.[9]

During the 1820s, Morrison sought to develop new sources of income. He built a water-powered sawmill and a distillery, the products of which he sold at his store in Kaskaskia. He also erected a toll bridge across the Kaskaskia River. The first attempt a little north of the village was washed away by a flood. A second attempt succeeded and operated until 1828, by which time construction and repair expenses had exceeded revenue, so the bridge was abandoned and soon collapsed.[10] Morrison also owned and leased two ferries on the Mississippi and dabbled in lead mining. The former brought in some money, but the latter led to losses. Morrison also bought slaves, eventually holding more than twenty. Those he purchased after 1807 were legally termed long-term "indentured servants," differing from chattel slaves only in name. After 1820, Morrison rented out the labor of many of his slaves.[11]

Throughout his life, Morrison acquired and accumulated land. Undoubtedly, he shared in the common opinion that equated landholding with the social status of a gentleman, and he probably saw in land a stability notably lacking in his commercial ventures. Morrison, like many of his contemporaries, paid little attention to legal formalities, and he acquired a reputation for questionable practices in his land deals. In 1804, Congress established a land office in Kaskaskia, the first task of which was to review all land claims in the district. Morrison claimed 193 parcels of land, consisting of 50,000 acres and 16 town lots. The land office rejected his claims to 27,400 acres: 11,200 acres on the bases of forgery and perjury and another 16,200 acres because of insufficient proof of title. Morrison did acquire title to an additional 1,619 acres he claimed in the Vincennes district, but his claims to 1,200 acres in Missouri were ruled invalid.

Despite having relatively diminished income after 1820, Morrison had enough accumulated wealth to live in a princely style. He was noted for his elegant dress and the fashionable appointments of his large home. When Lafayette visited Kaskaskia in 1825, Morrison gave a grand ball at his home in Lafayette's honor; and when in 1833 the sisters of Order of the Visitation arrived in Kaskaskia, Morrison extended hospitality and aid to them. William Morrison was raised a Quaker, but late in life, following the lead of his brother's wife, he converted to Catholicism. Upon his death in 1837, he was buried in the Catholic cemetery in Kaskaskia. In 1892, his remains and elegant tomb were moved to the Garrison Hill Cemetery (fig. 9.4).

Fig. 9.4. The funerary monument of William Morrison, Garrison Hill Cemetery, before it was damaged in 2009. Now all that remains is the slab, which sits forlornly flat on the ground, broken in three pieces. Photograph courtesy of David Ramsey.

SAVINIEN ST. VRAIN HOUSE

THE SAVINIEN ST. Vrain House was a Midwestern Federal house that departed from the formal Federal model in several regards (fig. 9.5). There were four windows on the second floor, where traditional Federal would have five, and two doors on the first floor, where one would be conventional. St. Vrain probably used one room of his house as an office, separate from the living area with its own entrance. The house was built on a freestone foundation and covered with clapboards, which allows for little speculation about its fundamental construction technique from surviving sketches. Savinien St. Vrain had seventeen children by two wives, and while all would not have been in residence at once, the house must nevertheless have been crowded.

The French aristocrat Pierre-Charles de Lassus de Luzières fled the revolution in his homeland, ultimately making his home at New Bourbon in what is now Missouri. He is the subject of an exemplary biography by Carl J. Ekberg.[12] His son, Jacques Marcellin Ceran de Hault de Lassus de St. Vrain, was Savinien St. Vrain's father.

Two of Savinien St. Vrain's older brothers were prominent. Charles de Hault de Lassus de Luzières was lieutenant governor of Upper Louisiana under the Spanish regime, and Ceran de Hault de Lassus de St.

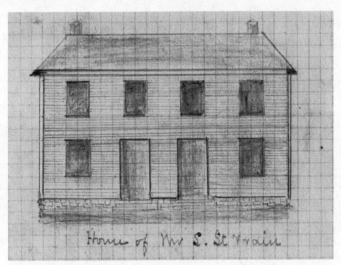

Fig. 9.5. Sketch of the home of S. St. Vrain by Mrs. H. S. Currie, circa 1865. Inscribed "House of Mr. S. St. Vrain." Courtesy of the Abraham Lincoln Presidential Library and Museum.

Vrain was a partner in Bent, St. Vrain, and Company, the traders who established the famous Bent's Fort and Fort St. Vrain in Colorado. Ceran St. Vrain also was a supplier for the army in the West and even became a newspaper editor.

Savinien St. Vrain was born near St. Louis in 1806 (fig. 9.6). He settled permanently in Kaskaskia in 1829 and in 1830 married Françoise Virginie Ménard, of the prominent Ménard family. They had nine children. Françoise died in 1853, and Savinien remarried in 1857, to Virginia Guthrie. They had eight more children.[13]

Savinien St. Vrain led an active political life.[14] He was elected assessor and treasurer of Randolph County, was three times sheriff, and served as circuit clerk for sixteen years. For much of his political career, Savinien St. Vrain was a Whig, and upon the effective dissolution of that party, he became a Democrat. For a brief time, he was the general manager of the *Picket Guard* newspaper in Chester, Illinois.

Originally founded in 1862 as the *Egyptian Picket Guard*, the newspaper soon suspended operations, apparently for financial reasons. Then a Democratic stock company purchased the paper and, in 1863, dropped *Egyptian* from the title. At this point, St. Vrain became the special agent, treasurer, and general manager. In July 1864, the paper's southern sympathies enraged a group of Union soldiers, who broke into

Fig. 9.6. Savinien St. Vrain. *An Illustrated Historical Atlas Map of Randolph County, Ills.* ([Edwardsville?], IL: W. R Brink, 1875), 56.

the newspaper and scattered the type in the streets, although they did not damage the press or severely damage the building. Other Copperhead newspapers in Illinois suffered much more severely.[15] The newspaper soon resumed operations, and a moderate proprietor took control. The newspaper underwent many changes in ownership in succeeding years, though generally retaining its Democratic orientation. In 1867, the name changed to *Valley Clarion*, and it continued to publish under that name until at least 1876.[16]

As the years passed and Kaskaskia declined, many of the prominent residents left, some moving to Ste. Geneviève, others to Chester. St. Vrain died at Chester in 1879.

THE FERDINAND MAXWELL HOUSE

THE MIDWESTERN FEDERAL house of Ferdinand Maxwell was apparently built of wood and covered with clapboards (fig. 9.7). Ferdinand Maxwell, 1812–1879, was the eldest son of Hugh Charles Maxwell and Marie Odile Ménard, the eldest daughter of Pierre Ménard.[17] After his father's death,

Fig. 9.7. Sketch of the Ferdinand Maxwell House by Mrs. H. S. Currie, circa 1865. Inscribed "Home Mr. Ferdinand Maxwell. Miss Evaline his second daughter was quite a beauty in the early sixties. She married Billie Morrison a nephew of Col. Jarrot." Courtesy of the Abraham Lincoln Presidential Library and Museum.

Ferdinand took over management of the family store in Kaskaskia, but by the time he assumed control, the lucrative days of Indian trade were passed. Ferdinand held a number of responsible posts in Kaskaskia in the decade from 1839 to 1849: clerk of the court of common pleas, county clerk, commissioner of roads, and registrar of the land office.[18]

Ferdinand's younger brother, Lucien Bonaparte Maxwell, went west at an early age and became vastly wealthy and powerful. In 1859, Ferdinand followed his brother west, where he became an Indian agent working with the Apaches and Utes.

G. W. STALEY HOUSE

THE G. W. Staley House was a Midwestern Federal residence of brick on a limestone foundation, reportedly built about 1816. A stone-built wing was later added to the back of the house, producing the L-shaped configuration typical of Folk Victorian farmhouses. The Staley home was the southernmost of the large houses in old Kaskaskia and the last one standing. The photograph in figure 9.8 was made in January 1906 and is

Fig. 9.8. G. W. Staley House. The photograph, showing the wing added to the back of the house, was taken in January 1906 by Miss Valentine Smith. Photograph in the Missouri History Museum, St. Louis.

probably the last photograph of a Kaskaskia building. At that time the house had just been abandoned, and the Mississippi, creeping ever closer, was expected to take the house that spring.

George W. Staley was born in Virginia in 1816. His father died when he was eight years old, so George left school early and apprenticed as a tailor. In 1837, he came to Kaskaskia, where he opened a tailor shop. In 1843, Staley married Harriet L. Feaman, born in Illinois in 1827. Harriet's father, Jacob Feaman, once operated the mill originally constructed by Prisque Pagé and later owned by General Edgar.[19]

In 1847, Staley expanded his business to a general store, called simply the Kaskaskia Store. Staley's business was largely retail, supplying consumers at Kaskaskia and the surrounding area. An advertisement from 1859 gives a good idea of the scope of the business (fig. 9.9).

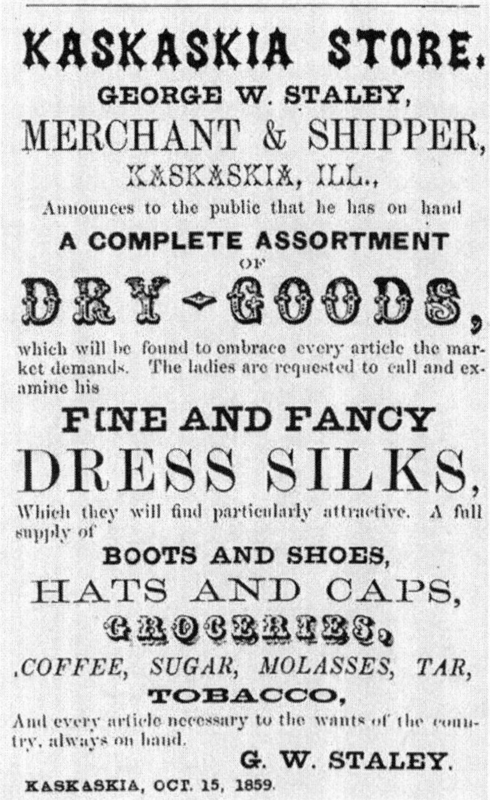

Fig. 9.9. Advertisement for G. W. Staley's Kaskaskia Store, 1859.
E. J. Montague, *A Directory, Business Mirror, and Historical Sketches of Randolph County* (Alton: Courier Steam, 1859), 122.

In 1850, Staley hired a young German immigrant, Gustave Pape, to clerk in his store. In 1861, Pape became Staley's partner in the store, and they continued in partnership until 1865, when Pape went into business for himself.[20] In 1867, Staley's Kaskaskia Store burned. Underinsured, he suffered a heavy loss. In 1870, Staley and family moved from Kaskaskia to Chester, where he established a tailor shop in partnership with Charles Wasseil. Harriet died in 1889, and George in 1901.

ANONYMOUS MIDWESTERN FEDERAL HOUSES

MIDWESTERN FEDERAL BUILDINGS stood on Elm Street. In the photograph of figure 9.10, each appears to have had four windows on the second story and just two symmetrically arranged windows on either side of a central door on the first story. The two farthest away appear to be brick structures with symmetrical double-wide chimneys at the gable ends. The closest is covered with clapboards, and the chimneys also differ, one double-width and the other single. The windows in the visible gable end of the house were boarded up at the time the photograph was taken. The house was probably partially or totally abandoned.

Fig. 9.10. Photograph labeled "View on principal street in Kaskaskia, Looking East. (Spots are flaws on camera film) Sept., 1891. W. G. E[ggleston]." Courtesy of the Abraham Lincoln Presidential Library and Museum.

Fig. 9.11. Parochial residence, Kaskaskia. Courtesy of the
Abraham Lincoln Presidential Library and Museum.

TWO ECLECTIC HOUSES

IN THE COURSE of the two centuries of Kaskaskia's existence, the parish
priest always had a residence, but there is little specific information about
the parochial residences (fig. 9.11). According to Sister Mary Josephine
Barber, when the sisters of the Order of the Visitation first went to Kaskaskia in 1833, the priest's residence was a humble house, "dilapidated,"
and containing "only two or three rooms."[21]

Later in the nineteenth century, the parishioners constructed the
last parochial residence of old Kaskaskia from bricks salvaged from the
sisters' academy, abandoned after the flood of 1844.[22] It was a late Midwestern Federal house built with a rear wing at a right angle to the main
block, a form popular in the Victorian era. A number of Midwestern
Federal homes in Kaskaskia added such wings during the nineteenth
century, but in this case the wing appears to be part of the original
construction. The earliest photograph (see fig. 5.6), from about 1878,
shows the house before the addition of the characteristically Victorian
porch apparent in later photographs. Note the lathe-turned and ornamented pillars.

Another eclectic building was probably a farmhouse originally but,
by 1887, served as a saloon and was vacant by 1893. The odd arrangement
of doors and windows indicates that the original building underwent

Fig. 9.12. Abandoned house, Kaskaskia, on the eve of destruction, circa 1898. Courtesy of the Abraham Lincoln Presidential Library and Museum.

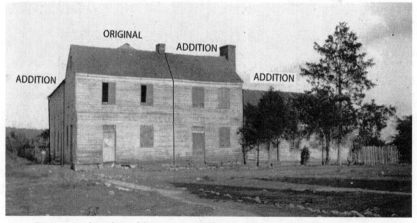

Fig. 9.13. Abandoned house, in a photograph inscribed "KASKASKIA, ILLS. This building was vacant in 1893. In 1887 it was a saloon operated by Bill Danis. Danis family (pronounced don-ee) was an old French family." Here, additions to the original structure are marked. Photograph in the Missouri History Museum, St. Louis.

extensive alterations and additions (fig. 9.12). The front of the building displays four windows on the second story asymmetrically positioned and two doors and two windows on the first floor, also asymmetrically arranged. The two chimneys are asymmetrically disposed as well, a smaller one near the middle of the roof and a much larger one at the far end. All suggest that the original construction was a modest Midwestern

Federal building with just two windows on the second floor and a door and single window on the first floor. The building was eventually extended twice laterally and by a wing added at a right angle at the rear (fig. 9.13).

There is a door in the gable end of the original core, apparently converted from a window. It is just around the corner from a door on the front of the house, and it probably led to an enclosed stairway to the second floor. The wing at the back of the house was entered by another door. This large house may have been home to a very large family or perhaps a family, servants, and farmhands, accommodated in rooms served by separate entrances, before it became a saloon late in its existence. At the time the first photograph was taken, the rear wing had begun to collapse into the Mississippi. The rest of the building must have soon followed.

PART 3

PSEUDO-FOLKLORE

CHAPTER 10

"THE CURSE OF KASKASKIA"— CREATIVE FICTION, NOT HISTORY

"THE CURSE OF Kaskaskia" is a tale existing in two major and many minor variations that attributes the destruction of the town to a curse. A clipping from an unidentified newspaper bearing the dateline Chester, Illinois, July 4, 1892, contains the earliest version of the story. The article records the dedication of the Garrison Hill Cemetery, where the bodies from the cemetery in old Kaskaskia were transferred as the Mississippi encroached on the old town, and then proceeds to recount the curse story as follows:

> ... the whole calamity of the downfall of Kaskaskia is said to be the fulfillment of a curse pronounced against the town in the seventeenth century by an outraged priest.
>
> The story of this remarkable priest and the curse has come down from father to son through a long line of old French settlers and inhabitants of the place, several of whom now reside in Chester.
>
> The legend or tradition runs like this: During the height of gayety and fashion holding sway, when Kaskaskia was a city of perhaps 10,000 people, the Bishop, hearing of the people's laxity in religious concerns, sent a conscientious and courageous priest there with instructions to inaugurate a new régime in the spiritual and moral condition of the dwellers in the Lord's vineyard. When the holy man reached his field of labor he was painfully surprised to discover that his services were sadly needed and that vigorous measures were

necessary, and he forthwith called a halt. He told his flock of their sins and laid the truth before them with such boldness and denunciation that his hearers, at first alarmed, murmured and next rebelled.

It was then that the priest laid on the lash of truth, and scored them so roundly that it soon became unbearable to the gay devotees of one pure shrine for the Sabbath and six other altars of varied hue the rest of the week, and they at length took the reverend gentleman by force to the shores of the Mississippi River, and putting him in an open shell of a boat, without oars or food, compass or guide, turned him adrift upon the murking [*sic*] waters, while the crowd, enflamed with excitement and drink, shouted in derision. It is said that as the boat drifted away from the bank the holy father stood up bareheaded, and with arms lifted toward the heavens, poured forth through pallid lips the most terrible curses his insulted and injured manhood could command.

He cursed the people in all degrees of life; he anathematized the fields and crops; he asked God to destroy and utterly obliterate the very ground upon which the people had built their homes, and wished that the river might flow across their gardens and carry them in grains of sand to the ocean. As long as his voice was audible and long after the black-robed figure had disappeared in the darkness of night his audience, now awed and hushed by his horrible words, held in silence his parting malediction. He never was seen or heard of again. The mob, feeling like murderers, told their children and grandchildren the strange story in the firm belief that the curse would be fulfilled.[1]

This is not genuine folklore, but rather journalistic fiction of recent origin masquerading as a genuine old tradition. The anonymous newspaper reporter places the story in the "seventeenth century." At the time the story was written, Kaskaskia was generally though incorrectly believed to have been settled in 1683, but the church register definitively shows Kaskaskia was not founded until 1703. The population of Kaskaskia never approached ten thousand. The earliest census, 1723, lists the French population as 196! During the French regime, Kaskaskia's population reached its greatest number on the eve of the French and Indian War. Even then, the census of 1752 records the population of Kaskaskia as only 671. Perhaps a few dozen transient voyageurs, traders, and hunters might be added to that number, but the census indicates the entire population of all the Illinois Country, even in 1752, did not approach ten thousand. In the period between 1810 and 1820, Kaskaskia reached its greatest size. The report to the statehood convention of 1818 gives the population of all Randolph County, of which Kaskaskia was by far the largest town, as 2,974. The federal census of 1820 lists 3,533 for the whole county.[2]

The story fails in still more damaging ways. The history of the Catholic Church in Kaskaskia is well attested in surviving records, the names and tenures of the officiating priests recorded.[3] There is no hint of any such event as recounted in this tall tale, the scandalous nature of which would have resounded loudly all the way to the court of the French king. Throughout the French regime, Kaskaskia seems to have been a quiet, conservative, pious French village. In the early years of American rule, one priest did denounce the people of Kaskaskia in harsh terms, the tumultuous and mentally unstable Father Pierre Huet de la Valinière, of the Society of Jesus. The Jesuit came to Illinois in 1786 and immediately began to quarrel with virtually everyone, a pattern that characterized all of his career. La Valinière so alienated the people of Kaskaskia that they sent a complaint to Congress detailing his irrational and offensive behavior. Although he seems an ideal character for the inhabitants of Kaskaskia to have set adrift on the river, he left Illinois of his own volition in 1789 and died in Canada in 1806.[4] The murdered priest of the story is complete fiction.

The curse story appeared again but in much different form in the *Chicago Inter-Ocean* on February 3, 1901:

> As the story goes, Jean Bernard came to this country from France in 1689, bringing with him his wife and 10-year-old daughter Marie. The family settled in Kaskaskia where Bernard established a merchandise business. The Frenchman soon became one of the prosperous and influential men of the town. Marie grew to be a beautiful woman, much courted by the most eligible young men of the new country. She was in no hurry to accept any of them, and her fame as a belle spread from Lake Michigan to the Gulf of Mexico.
>
> A young chief of the Kaskaskia tribe of Indians having become converted to Christianity, after several years of study under the tutelage of the Jesuits, built himself a house in Kaskaskia, and was taken into partnership in one of the trading houses there. He was prosperous, handsome and well educated, and was soon received into

the homes of the white settlers. One night at a ball he happened to meet Marie Bernard.

The girl was at once fascinated by the tall, fine-looking Indian, who fell in love with her at first sight and made no secret of his admiration. But Bernard soon noticed the attachment and forbade his daughter from communicating with the young Indian. To be sure that there would be no more meetings, Bernard used his influence to prevent the chief from attending any of the social entertainments given in Kaskaskia.

But love always finds a way, and the young couple managed to see each other despite all the precautions of the girl's father. But Bernard became aware of these meetings, and again took means to prevent them. He was a man of wealth and influence, and he had the Indian forced out of his partnership in the trading company.

The Indian left Kaskaskia, and for almost a year nothing was heard from him. Bernard thought that his daughter had forgotten her love, for she appeared gay and careless and accepted with apparent pleasure the attentions of a young Frenchman. One night when a large ball at Kaskaskia was at its height, Marie Bernard disappeared.

Those who searched for Marie discovered that the young chief of the Kaskaskians had been seen that evening in town, and the conclusion was at once reached that the girl had eloped with him. Bernard at once organized a party to go in pursuit of the fugitives. As there was a heavy snow on the ground their trail was easily discovered and followed. The Indian and Marie had crept away on foot, and as the pursuers were supplied with fast horses, the young lovers were captured after a day's chase, about forty miles from Kaskaskia. Their destination had been the French settlement of St. Louis, where the Indian had provided a home for his wife.

The Indian surrendered without resistance, and the posse started on the journey back to Kaskaskia. Most of the men who composed Bernard's party wanted to kill the Indian instantly, but Bernard would not allow it, for, he said, they should leave him to deal with his daughter's love.

When the party reached Kaskaskia, the girl was placed in a convent there. Then Bernard took the Indian to the bank of the Mississippi, and binding him tightly to a log, turned him adrift in the river. As the helpless Indian floated away to his death he raised his eyes to heaven and cursed Bernard, who, he declared, would die a violent death. The Indian's last words were a prophesy that within 200 years the waters which were then bearing him away would sweep from the earth every vestige of the town, so that only the name would remain.

The unhappy girl died in the convent. Bernard was killed in 1712 in a duel. The last of Kaskaskia's soil will soon have been swallowed by the turbid waters, and the superstitious declare that the Indian's curse has had something to do with the passing of the once flourishing town. On dark stormy nights the ghost of the Indian is said to appear. The specter with strong arms bound and face upturned floats slowly on the river where the stream sweeps by the vanishing city in which Marie Bernard once lived, and in which she died mourning the red man whom she loved.[5]

The identical story appeared in the *Inter-Ocean* (Chicago) on February 3, 1901; *Jonesboro Gazette* (Jonesboro, Illinois) on March 2, 1901; the *True Republican* (Sycamore, Illinois) on March 23, 1901; and probably in a number of other papers as well. Such stories were frequently copied from one paper to another.

This second curse story, much more romantic than the first, has become the dominant version, reproduced on many websites, with various abbreviations, additions, and distortions. Marie becomes Maria. Jean Bernard loses his first name. The Indian acquires a name, Ampakaya. The date shifts from before 1712 to 1735, without explanation. Details vary apparently at random. Online versions often cite no source, though occasionally one refers to another online source. All obviously stem from the 1901 account, more or less modified and corrupted. None exhibit any attempt to examine the story critically.[6]

Even in the original form, the account contains obvious nonsense. Jean Bernard supposed came from France in 1689 and settled in Kaskaskia, founded in 1703. According to the story, Marie Bernard was born in 1679. Marie and her Indian lover were supposedly fleeing to St. Louis when intercepted, and, of course, St. Louis was not founded until 1764. Marie was allegedly placed in a convent at Kaskaskia. There was indeed a convent at Kaskaskia, but it was established in 1833, by which time Marie would have been 154 years old.

Jean Bernard was supposedly killed in a duel. France outlawed dueling in the seventeenth century, but despite the prohibition, duels continued to be fought. During the seventeenth and eighteenth centuries, however, dueling was exclusively an aristocratic practice. Jean Bernard, depicted as a bourgeois merchant, did not belong to the dueling class in the early eighteenth century, and no bourgeois duels are recorded at all in eighteenth-century French Illinois. Only early in the early nineteenth century were merchants considered gentlemen and engaged in duels.

In the early eighteenth century, Kaskaskia was a small village consisting of the Kaskaskia Indians, a couple of Jesuit missionaries, and a small number of largely transient voyageurs and traders, a few of whom were settling down and developing farms. The story's depiction of Kaskaskia as the site of prosperous merchant and trading houses again reflects the early nineteenth rather than the early eighteenth century.

Even more damning is the complete absence of any trace of Jean or Marie Bernard at Kaskaskia or anywhere else. Of course, not all documents from the eighteenth century have survived, but an amazingly large number have. There is no mention of Jean or Marie Bernard in the more than six thousand documents of the Kaskaskia Manuscripts, and they are not to be found in any of the other extensive collections of French Illinois documents and genealogical sources.[7] The mass of sources ought to contain some mention of Jean Bernard, a "prosperous and influential" businessman, and Marie Bernard, a beauty famed "from Lake Michigan to the Gulf of Mexico," if they actually existed. Many individuals of lesser status appear repeatedly. The Indian Ampakaya is equally unknown beyond the story.

In 1893, the year after the story of the bitter priest appeared in a newspaper, yet another form of the curse story made its way into Elizabeth Holbrook's *Old 'Kaskia Days: A Novel.* Local writers hold the work in high regard, and some have even cited Holbrook's description of the flood of 1844, which occurred before her birth, as if it were a primary historical source. In an imaginary scene, the author introduces the following snippet of conversation:

> "I say we are going to have Noah's flood," said old Madame Latulippe. "The people are wicked, and they play and dissipate. They will not listen to Father St. Cyr when he reproves them. We shall all perish, all perish." And she rocked back and forth.
>
> "No, no," said Basyl Taumur.
>
> "I say it. Father St. Cyr was seen on the top of Garrison Hill, standing by the old fort with his hands spread out toward old 'Kaskia,

and he cursed us with this great flood. Toinette said it. We shall all perish—shall perish."[8]

There is no further reference in the novel to the supposed curse, and it is apparent that the scene is entirely fictional. Holbrook calls the priest Donatien St. Cyr,[9] but his actual name was John Mary Irenæus St. Cyr, and he was a poor model for the unnamed priest of the curse story. Not only did he live over a century later, but he was, by all accounts, a kindly, considerate, and popular priest. On July 4, 1844, he wrote in the Immaculate Conception Parish register of marriages and burials an account of the "destructive rise" of the water that inundated Kaskaskia, which he calmly reported as a natural disaster. St. Cyr died peacefully long thereafter, in 1883, at the age of eighty.[10]

Holbrook and the newspaper writers may have drawn on an older, vague tradition of a curse on Kaskaskia. Sister Mary Josephine Barber, who recorded the history of the Order of the Visitation's convent at Kaskaskia, recounts that when the sisters first arrived in 1833, they stayed with the William Morrison family. There she observed that the Morrison home, which she termed a "stone mansion, the only real building in the place," had a fissure in a wall and wavy, uneven floors due to the earthquakes of 1811 and 1812. Sister Mary Josephine records that the locals said this was a manifestation of a curse on Kaskaskia, "but Madam R. Morrison told us she had heard some say, and hoped it was true, that Kaskaskia was cursed only for a certain number of years, and that the term of the malediction, having now expired, [the town] would revive from its long period of calamity and misery."[11]

Eliza Chambers, a graduate from the convent's Ménard Young Ladies' Academy in 1843, also made reference to the curse in a letter to her sister Mrs. Joseph H. LaMotte, written shortly after the Kaskaskia River flood and following epidemic in 1844: "Poor Kaskaskia! How truly a curse has fallen on it, as prophesied."[12] Neither of these mentions of a curse makes any reference to the Mississippi or to the elaborate stories that later appeared in the newspapers.

According to Father Benedict Roux, pastor of Kaskaskia from 1835 to 1839, it was Father Pierre Gibault, active throughout Illinois from 1768 to 1793, who pronounced what Roux called a "famous" prophecy: "This place shall be always furnished with priests, but none shall stay long. Its inhabitants shall contend with their cattle for the last ear of corn." Roux records the pronouncement without context.[13] Rather than a curse, the quotation appears to be a fragment of Gibault's lament over the condition of Kaskaskia during the darkest days of 1780s. A petition from the citizens of Kaskaskia to Major Jean-François (John Francis) Hamtramck expresses much the same sentiment in greater detail:

> Our horses, horned cattle & corn are stolen & destroyed without the power of making any effective resistance: Our houses are in ruins & decay; our lands are uncultivated; debtors absconded and absconding, our little commons destroyed. We are apprehensive of a dearth of corn and our best prospects are misery and distress, or what is more probable an untimely death by the hands of savages. . . . The greater part of our citizens have left the country on this account to reside in the Spanish dominions; others are now following.[14]

Conditions were such that even the dedicated Father Gibault left Illinois to cross over to New Madrid on the Spanish side of the Mississippi, where he continued his ministry until his death in 1802.

Sister Mary Josephine Barber, Eliza Chambers, and Father Benedict Roux mention the notion of a curse in vague and general terms, referring to the general decline of the town. The claim that Kaskaskia was cursed to be destroyed by the Mississippi appears nowhere until 1892, by which time the Mississippi had already destroyed much of the town and was destroying the rest. The Mississippi did not begin to shift course toward Kaskaskia until the mid-1860s,[15] and the threat to Kaskaskia was apparent to no one before that shift substantially ate into the eastern side of the river in the 1870s. In 1892, the date of the first story, graves were moved from Kaskaskia to the new cemetery on Garrison Hill, and by 1901, date of the second story, the last traces of old Kaskaskia were fast disappearing.

There is a simple explanation for the curse stories. In the nineteenth and early years of the twentieth century, long before electronic transmission disseminated information broadly and rapidly, newspaper editors frequently found it difficult to fill their pages. As local news was often insufficient, they turned to whatever they could find or create. The folklorist Arthur K. Moore describes these practices as

> owing in large measure to the catholicity of taste possessed by many a whimsical editor and to lack of adequate sources of conventional

news. Editors permitted themselves wide latitude in supplying . . .
a *mélange* of imitative verse by hometown muses, sketches of local
characters, reports of traditional observances, superstitions, and
prejudices and fabulous narratives.[16]

During the late nineteenth and early twentieth centuries, many journalists, politicians, orators, and even those who styled themselves histori-
ans wrote about the past, not to produce an objective understanding of
events, but rather to create mythic stories that evoked emotions, promoted values, earned money, or even just entertained. Such writers felt
free to imagine, enhance, distort, and even create anew. The examples
multiply, ranging from Parson Weems's oft-repeated phony account of
Washington's childhood to the underground city supposedly discovered
by coal miners 360 feet beneath Moberly, Missouri. The account of the
underground city was published in the local newspaper on, suggestively,
the first of April 1885, despite which it is still taken seriously by some. In
Illinois we have cases such as the false Starved Rock massacre of 1769
and the egregious falsehoods of John F. Snyder, president of the Illinois
Historical Society, whose long article "Captain John Baptiste Saucier at
Fort Chartres in Illinois, 1751–1763," published in the *Transactions of the
Illinois State Historical Society* in 1919, is a complete fraud and has long
since been exposed as such.[17] Newspaper editors, urgently needing to
fill blank pages, were particularly inclined to accept and even promote
such fictions, which at that time were usually recognized as such and not
taken seriously. In regard to Kaskaskia, journalists imaginatively took the
common motif of a righteous man condemned by a corrupt crowd or of
tragic lovers doomed by an enraged father and combined it with a vague
tradition of a curse, anachronistic bits of Kaskaskia's half-remembered
past, and the Mississippi's contemporary destruction of the town.

In the years to come the "Curse of Kaskaskia" was revived sporadi-
cally, often with novel additions and distortions, to fill newspaper columns. In 1928, the *Sparta News-Plaindealer* published a story jumbling
together elements from Elizabeth Holbrook's novel and the story of the
drowned priest. According to this version, it was St. Cyr who was sent
to a watery grave in the river "more than a hundred years ago." The article quotes the curse at length, no source cited, and adds that the curse
rested on Kaskaskia for four generations and was now ending. In 1962,
the *Sparta News-Plaindealer* again revived the story, this time in the

context of disputes over whether Kaskaskia Island should be linked by a bridge to Missouri or Illinois and whether Beaver Island, a recent alluvial deposit of the Mississippi covering much of the area of old Kaskaskia, should belong to Illinois or Missouri. The article mentions both versions of the curse and names "Father St. Cyrs" (note the variant spelling) as the drowned priest. Neither article cites sources nor makes any attempt to inquire into the origin of the curse stories; both are fillers, stories used to fill empty space in a newspaper.[18]

The "Curse of Kaskaskia" stories have historical significance, but they do not recount historical realities. Rather, they are journalistic fictions, short stories, akin to the novels by Catherwood, Holbrook, and Fessended that appeared at about the same time. As such they may be appreciated, but when presented without context, they sometimes mislead readers.[19]

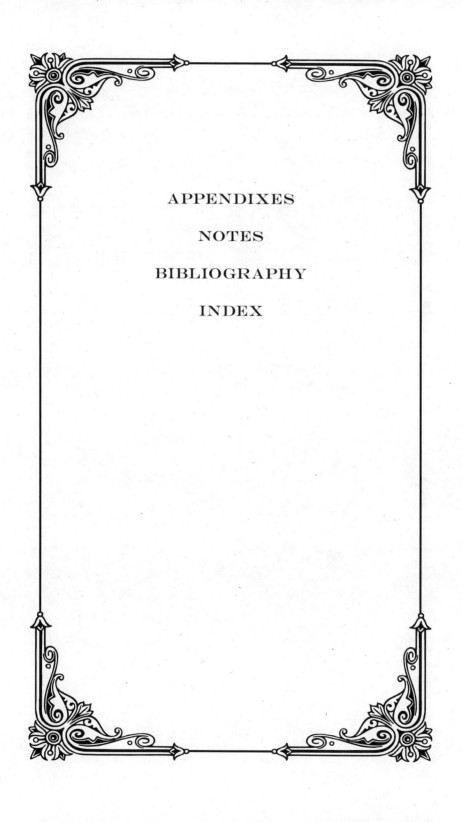

APPENDIXES

NOTES

BIBLIOGRAPHY

INDEX

APPENDIX A

NOTES ON PHOTOGRAPHERS AND SKETCH ARTISTS

PHOTOGRAPHS AND SKETCHES of Kaskaskia survive in a number of places. Some are scattered throughout various publications. Others are in collections of great midwestern libraries: the Abraham Lincoln Presidential Library and Museum, Springfield, Illinois (formerly the Illinois State Historical Library); the Chicago History Museum, Chicago, Illinois; and the Missouri History Museum Library and Research Center, St. Louis, Missouri. The Chester Public Library and the Randolph County Museum and Archives also preserve a few photos, including several not found anywhere else. Photographs and sketches generally came to these institutions as donations, on occasion from the artists themselves, other times from individuals who found them in family albums or other accumulations of keepsakes.

Often photographs are identified by notes in the margin or on the back, but such notes are not always accurate. For instance, General Edgar's house in Kaskaskia was certainly reduced to ruins, probably by fire, in the mid-nineteenth century, but photographs taken around 1900 incorrectly identify several different extant buildings as General Edgar's house. Notes on different prints of the same picture sometimes bear conflicting identifications. Even photographs published by reputable scholars must be examined critically. In *Deep Roots*, Faherty identifies a photograph as "The Church of the Immaculate Conception in Kaskaskia, built in 1799" (15), but the building is actually the Cahokia vertical-log church, photographed before the nineteenth-century clapboard siding was removed.

Unlabeled photographs from different locations, particularly Kankakee, are sometimes mixed in with photographs of old Kaskaskia, and photographs of new Kaskaskia are often not distinguished from photographs of the old town. Except for a few photographs of new Kaskaskia, clearly labeled as such, we include only photographs of old Kaskaskia and exclude dubious attributions. For example, a utility pole is visible in the background of an old photograph of a feed store and boarding stable. As no certain photographs of old Kaskaskia show electrical or telephone poles, we conclude that the photograph is of new Kaskaskia rather than the old town.

Not every photograph of Kaskaskia is included here. There are many repetitive photographs of the old Kaskaskia State House; only a couple of the best are included here. Some photographs are too poorly preserved for reproduction; others are simply not visually interesting or informative enough to warrant inclusion. For instance, one photograph shows the nondescript back of the "New Hotel," but apparently no one photographed the front of the building!

PHOTOGRAPHERS AND ILLUSTRATORS

MARIE CZACH, IN *A Directory of Early Illinois Photographers*, provides information about some photographers, but the directory is incomplete and deals only with professional photographers. By the late nineteenth century, there were significant numbers of amateur photographers. More information can be gleaned from notes on the backs or margins of photographs.

Hiram Williams Beckwith (1833–1903) was the son of a founder of Danville, Illinois. He studied law in the Danville office of Ward Hill Lamon and Abraham Lincoln and was admitted to the bar in 1854. He moved to Bloomington, Illinois, in 1859 and five years later entered into a partnership with Raymond W. Hanford, another well-respected jurist. Beckwith became a judge before retiring from the law in 1876. Beckwith devoted the rest of his life to the history of Illinois and the old Northwest Territory. He was president of the board of trustees of the Illinois State Historical Library and left behind a rich heritage of publications, including a panoramic photograph of Kaskaskia that he took in 1895 and published in Beckwith, "General George Roger Clark's Conquest of the Illinois," following page 200.

Mrs. H. S. Currie wrote a letter to Clarence W. Alvord, which is now at the University of Illinois Library, Abraham Lincoln and Illinois collection, in Urbana. Inscribed on letterhead from her husband's business, the body of the letter is handwritten:

> *H. S. Currie*
> *Real Estate, Loans and Insurance*
> *229 South Ave.*
>
>   Pueblo, Colorado_____190__
>
> Prof Alvord
>   Dr Sir
>
> I having indirectly heard of your great interest in the town of
> Kaskaskia and of everything pertaining to the memories of

the old village. I thought you might care to have some rude sketches of the homes and places as they appeared forty years ago. I have from time to time made these pictures; while they have no artistic merit they ought to have some historic value. I enclose a couple that you may judge of them. I have the old convent, residence of Judge Pope, Bond place, Sen. Kane's Kaskaskia Hotel, and several others. I should like to dispose of them. If they are of any value you can advise me. As to my integrity I can refer you to the Koerner family, Mrs. Charles W. Thomas, widow of late Judge C. W. Thomas, and Hon. E. L. Thomas all of Belleville Ill.

Respectfully
Mrs. H. S. Currie
17 Block St.
Pueblo, Colorado

I spent twenty years
of my life in Kaskaskia

Mrs. Currie provided twelve sketches. The handwriting on the letter is identical to that on the sketches. In the 1950s, Marguerite Jenison Pease transferred eleven sketches to what is now the Abraham Lincoln Presidential Library, Springfield. The twelfth, a near duplicate of one of those in Springfield, remains at Urbana. Internal evidence as well as the letter above indicates that the sketches were made between 1860 and 1865.

In the few instances where Mrs. Currie's sketches can be compared to photographs, her proportions are inaccurate. She exaggerated the size of windows and doors, making buildings appear smaller than they were. Nevertheless, her sketches provide us with the only images of the homes of leading figures of Illinois in the early nineteenth century and the only view we have of the Kaskaskia home of a free African American.

Tina Fanetti is the author of a blog (viewfrombackpew.blogspot.com). She has visited and taken excellent photographs of notable Catholic churches throughout the Midwest. We thank her for permission to use her photos of the current church in new Kaskaskia.

William Green Eggleston (1859–1937), born in Virginia, earned a medical degree but became a writer and photographer. He first edited medical journals, but then he became involved in newspaper work in Illinois and Montana. In September 1891, Eggleston took a series of pictures in and around Kaskaskia. According to the state historical library, as recorded in Weber, *Alphabetic Catalog*, Eggleston presented a set of thirty-four photographs and "pen drawings of Kaskaskia and the Kaskaskia and Mississippi rivers, previous to 1896, and after the 'cut-off' of 1886 [*sic*]" (1881 is correct) to the Illinois State Historical Library (151–52). Eighteen of those photographs identified as Eggleston's by his notations in the margins are still present in the library, as are other photographs that agree with the brief descriptions in Weber's *Alphabetic Catalog* but that lack written attribution to Eggleston. The pen drawings cannot be located in the library.

Eggleston also edited and published newspapers at Helena, Montana, and in 1913 he moved to California, where he also edited a newspaper. He died in California in 1937. Eggleston advocated for a number of political and economic reforms, and his papers, primarily concerned with political matters, are in the Bancroft Library in Berkeley.

Max (probably Maximilian) von Fragstein, a member of an old German family, was a professional photographer operating out of Chester. Polk, in the *Illinois State Gazetteer and Business Directory*, on pages unnumbered, lists M. von Fragstein as a photographer in Chester. The anonymously authored *Historical and Descriptive Review of Illinois* indicates that "Max Fragstein" sold his photograph gallery, "an old established business," to Oliver Howard about 1893 (32–33). Fragstein seems to have been a typical photographer of his time, with much of his work consisting of family pictures.

Mrs. Charles L. French of Belleville (née Maude Roxana Crisler) and her sister, Miss Rose S. Crisler of Chester, visited Kaskaskia sometime in the late 1890s, and Mrs. French sketched buildings of old Kaskaskia. Five sketches and a short account of the visit were published in the *St. Louis Republican* newspaper, December 23, 1900, in the magazine section (35). To their published identifications listed below, we appended parenthetical corrections where needed:

1. "The Home of General Edgar" (actually the Col. Sweet Hotel)
2. "The First Executive Mansion in Illinois, Residence of Governor Bond"
3. "The Ruin of Riley's Stone Mill, the Oldest in the West" (actually the François Vallé *fils* mill on Dodge Creek south of Ste. Geneviève)
4. "The Old Mill, another view of the Riley Mill ruins" (actually the François Vallé *fils* mill on Dodge Creek south of Ste. Geneviève)
5. "The Land Office at Kaskaskia"

The anonymously authored "Last Years of Kaskaskia" includes a letter, evidently undated, from Maude French describing the visit. Though not realized at the time of publication, the letter is identical to the 1900 article, with the exception of a few minor omissions. Two new sketches by M. C. French appear with the letter (233, 237):

1. "The Menard Family Coach"
2. "An Old Home at Kaskaskia"

French's sketches are of less value than they first appear. French made her sketches from photographs rather than directly from her observations during the visit, and she misidentified the subjects of several of her sketches. The Shadrach Bond House was demolished in 1892, and French acknowledged that it had been destroyed before her visit. She misidentified the Col. Sweet Hotel as the house of "Gen. Edgar." The hotel had fallen into the river before French's visit, and she noted that nothing was left of it but a few stones at the time of her visit. The actual house of General John Edgar was destroyed, apparently reduced to a few charred timbers, long before her visit. The land office sketch comes from the left half of a photograph of the land office and bank published in G. W. Smith, *A History of Southern Illinois*, volume 1 (410), also surviving in several individual original prints. The Mississippi had also claimed the land office by the time of her visit. French misidentified two sketches as ruins of Riley's Mill, but actually they are sketches of the ruinous mill that belonged to Vallé south of Ste. Geneviève in Missouri. Again, these sketches were probably derived from photographs.

J. G. Miller was the rector of St. Mark Episcopal Church in Chester and an amateur photographer. The church was formed in 1843 and disbanded in 1955. An index of the sacraments administered by the church is available from the Randolph County Genealogical Society. Miller took photographic views of Kaskaskia at the end of the nineteenth century.

David Ramsey has been documenting southern Illinois locations in photography for most of his life. Many parks and historical locations in and around Randolph County are his favorite places to visit. Hundreds of his photos are featured on Google Earth. Most recently, volunteering for Findagrave.com has been a fascinating way of exploring his family history or that of others from his hometown of Chester, Illinois: "Southern Illinois has a rich history, especially in Randolph County. It's amazing that we live among these historical sites, and that many of them still exist and are used even today. To me, history is like time travel" (personal communication). David attended the University of Phoenix, where he graduated with a bachelor's degree in elementary education. We thank him for his generous permission to use his photographs of the Garrison Hill Cemetery and the William Morrison grave before its monument was damaged in 2009.

John A. Scholten (1829–1894) was a prominent photographer in St. Louis. His advertisements indicate that he won many awards for his work. In 1877, Scholten accompanied a committee of the Missouri Historical Society to take pictures during a visit to Kaskaskia. The visit and his participation are recorded in the *St. Louis Republican* newspaper of July 19, 1877, reprinted in the *Fair Play* newspaper (Ste. Geneviève, MO), August 2, 1877 (2–3). The newspaper article mentions that Scholten took photographs that apparently have not survived (or at least that we have not been able to locate). Two of the photographs taken by Scholten in 1877 served as the basis for engravings in the anonymously authored "Kaskaskia, the Old French Capital of Illinois."

Larry Senalik was born in 1953. He earned an MS from the University of Illinois at Urbana-Champaign. He has served as information technology professional at the Illinois Department of Public Health, senior public services administrator at the Illinois Department of Healthcare and Family Services, and information technology auditor at the Illinois State Employees Retirement System. He is a talented photographer with thousands of photographs available for view on Flickr. We thank him for his photograph of the Ménard monument on the Springfield capitol grounds.

Thomas Smith is listed in the 1882, 1884, 1886, and 1888 editions of Polk, *Illinois State Gazetteer*, as a professional photographer operating in Chester. His photograph, dated 1884, of the Pierre Ménard House, not included here, is one of the earliest images of Kaskaskia. It is published in Mason, *Early Illinois and Chicago*, and survives in a separate individual print in the Chicago History Museum. The margins of the photo are badly out of focus and distorted, but no such distortion is apparent in Smith's photograph of the much-altered Kane house on the bluffs across the Kaskaskia River, not included here, also in the Chicago History Museum.

L. J. Smith took photographs of Kaskaskia in the late 1890s, mainly of the old Kaskaskia State House. He is not listed in Czach's *Directory* and was probably an amateur photographer.

Miss Valentine Smith made the latest photographs of old Kaskakia, in January 1906. By that time, little was left of the town, only a few buildings in what had been the extreme southern part of town. The prints of her photographs tend to be poorly preserved, either because the developing chemicals were not properly neutralized or the black backing material on which she mounted the photographs has damaged the images. This is especially unfortunate as it is apparent that Miss Smith was a talented photographer. From a prominent Chicago family, Valentine Smith was active in the Chicago Historical Society and was, at one time in the early twentieth century, the official archivist of Chicago.

A. L. Steles took a notable picture of the Kaskaskia State House in 1898 as it began to collapse, according to a handwritten attribution on the back of the photo, which is kept in the Abraham Lincoln Presidential Library in Springfield. He too is not listed in Czach's *Directory* and was probably an amateur photographer.

Dr. David Taylor obtained his PhD in physics from the University of Maryland in 1983. After six years of working at the *Physical Review* (a physics research journal), he joined the faculty at Northwestern University in 1989 and has been there ever since. He is interested in Victorian architecture and takes photos of striking and interesting Victorian houses. His website Victorian Houses contains an excellent collection of photos with captions that illustrate variations in Victorian style.

APPENDIX B

LEXICON

Appentis. A lean-to or shed attached to a main building.

Arpent. French unit of both linear and land-area measurement, roughly equaling 192 feet or 0.85 acre, respectively.

Bousillage. A mixture of clay and grass or other fibrous material used to fill gaps between timbers in French vertical-timber buildings. See also *pierrotage*.

Cahokia. A tribe sharing language and culture with the Kaskaskia and a number of other tribes that formed the alliance known collectively as the Illinois.

Gallerie. French for "porch." During the late eighteenth century, French colonial houses in the Illinois Country often incorporated galleries on one, two, three, or four sides. Later Franco-American-style homes usually had just one gallerie on the front.

Kaskaskia Manuscripts. A collection of over six thousand documents dating from 1714 to 1816, mainly in French, brought together at Kaskaskia and later transferred to Chester. The documents are predominantly notarial transactions such as sales, leases, deeds, depositions, labor contracts, marriage contracts, and wills. They form a chief source for the history of early Illinois.

Marguillier. Lay churchwarden responsible for the administration of church property.

Michigamea. A tribe sharing language and culture with the Kaskaskia and a number of other tribes that formed the alliance known collectively as the Illinois.

Peoria. A tribe sharing language and culture with the Kaskaskia and a number of other tribes that formed the alliance known collectively as the Illinois.

Pierrotage. A mixture of clay and stones used to fill gaps between timbers in French vertical-timber buildings. See also *bousillage*.

Pimiteoui. Indian and French settlement at the site of modern-day Peoria.

Poteaux en terre. French construction technique of building walls by placing timbers vertically in a trench and filling the gaps between the timbers with materials such as clay and grass or clay and stones. See *bousillage* and *pierrotage.*

Poteaux sur sol. French construction technique of building walls by mortising vertical timbers into timber sills and head plates and filling the areas between the vertical timbers with materials such as clay and grass or clay and stones. See *bousillage* and *pierrotage.*

Tamaroa. A tribe sharing language and culture with the Kaskaskia and a number of other tribes that formed the alliance known collectively as the Illinois.

Voyageur. From the French word for "traveler," the voyageur was a boatman who moved goods by the waterways and portages that connected the French settlements in America.

NOTES

1. DAWN OF KASKASKIA, 1673–1719

1. For the history of the Kaskaskia tribe before settling in southern Illinois in 1703, see Alvord, *Illinois Country*, 54–132.

2. The basic and enduring treatment of French Kaskaskia, originally published in 1948, is Belting, *Kaskaskia under the French Regime*. The name Kaskaskia, like so many other names, was spelled in many different ways, from Cascasquias to Kuskuskes. Sometimes, particularly in speech, it was shortened to Kaskia and even just Kas. In popular parlance the Kaskaskia River was frequently called the Okaw, from the pronunciation of the French "au 'Kas."

3. Pénicaut, *Fleur de Lys*, 137–39.

4. Peoria.

5. Pénicaut echoes the Jesuit claims about the conversion of the Kaskaskia. Diron d'Artaguiette, the inspector general of Louisiana who visited Kaskaskia in 1723, was less impressed: "The Jesuit fathers who have for more than thirty years been among them, have up to the present failed in their attempts to make them understand that God had made himself man and died for us." Diron d'Artaguiette, "Journal," in Mereness, *Travels*, 71.

6. Caddo.

7. Reyling, *Historical Kaskaskia*, 29.

8. In 1726, the Jesuits attempted to get recompense from the Compagnie des Indes for expenses incurred in building a new church and Jesuit residence at Indian Kaskaskia. As part of their argument, they stated that Boisbriand instigated the separation of the communities. Archives Nationales d'Outre-Mer, C13A.10.106. The Jesuit interpretations of events tend to be self-serving and not always entirely candid. They may have requested and encouraged Boisbriand's action and then omitted mention of that.

9. Ekberg, *Stealing Indian Women*, 24–30 and literature cited therein; White, *Wild Frenchmen*, 33–142.

10. Reyling, *Historical Kaskaskia*, 24.

11. Belting, *Kaskaskia*, 33.

2. FRENCH AND INDIAN KASKASKIAS, 1719–1765

1. Alphabet Laffilard, ANC C13A.8.226–226v; Belting, *Kaskaskia*, 13.

2. Diron d'Artaguiette, "Journal," in Mereness, *Travels*, 67–68. This was Diron's second trip to Illinois; on his first, he had accompanied Boisbriand, first commandant of Illinois, who arrived in 1719. At that time Diron took compass readings that resulted in the map.

3. Kaskaskia River.

4. Diron d'Artaguiette, "Journal," in Mereness, *Travels*, 67–68.

5. Familysearch.org, Kaskaskia Parish Records, First Book, p. 21 of the whole, second folio marked 8 at top of page.

6. Alphabet Laffilard, ANC C13A.10.225.

7. Maudell, *Census Tables*, "Census of the Inhabitants of Illinois Dated January 1, 1732," excerpt on Kaskaskia, 152–53.

8. Ekberg, *Colonial Ste. Genevieve*, 144–58.

9. The standard work on agriculture in French Illinois is Ekberg, *French Roots*.

10. Brown, *Voyageur*.

11. Alphabet Laffilard, ANC B70.472–473; Belting, *Kaskaskia*, 25–27.

12. Belting, *Kaskaskia*, 73–79.

13. Ekberg and Pregaldin, "Marie Rouensa-8cate8a."

14. Louis Turpin: Belting, *Kaskaskia*, 22, 25, 37, 58, 61, 79, 80, 90–91. Jacques Bourdon: Belting, *Kaskaskia*, 15, 20, 33, 43–44, 48–49, 66. The Kaskaskia Manuscripts contain abundant citations of both men's economic activity.

15. Kaskaskia Manuscripts.

16. De Berardinis, "1752 French Census," 195–203.

17. The name of the founder of the water mill was spelled several different ways, a frequent occurrence in the eighteenth and nineteenth centuries. His first name appears variously as Pax or Prix and the family name as Pagi, Page, and Paget. The parish records of Kaskaskia contain what is surely the best form of the name: Prisque Pagé. He married Marie-Françoise Michel on February 2, 1751. His sister later married Philippe-François de Rocheblave, who in his varied career served as a French officer of the marines and town commandant of Kaskaskia, the Spanish commandant of Ste. Geneviève, and the last British governor of Illinois. Prisque Pagé and his wife had three children born between 1760 and 1763, the last shortly before his death. Belting, *Kaskaskia*, 83, 91, 98.

Much misinformation surrounds the Pagé mill. The assertion that this was the earliest mill in Illinois, established before 1709, is contrary to documentary sources. Montague, *Directory*, 51–52, dates the origin of the mill much too early, but his remarks are clearly mere rhetorical speculation in the absence of fact. A number of imprudent writers have adopted Montague's words as fact.

18. Pittman, *Present State*, 85; Montague, *Directory*, 52, writes that the attackers were Kickapoo.

3. KASKASKIA AND INDIAN KASKASKIA UNDER BRITISH AND EARLY AMERICAN RULE, 1765–1790

1. Ekberg and Person, *St. Louis Rising*.

2. Morrissey, *Empire*, 209–32.

3. The "rock of Peorya" is modern Starved Rock, so called here because of the periodic occupation of the site by the Peoria tribe.

4. Pittman, *Present State*, 42–43.

5. Such enclosures were called, in French, *pieux en terre*, stakes in earth, or *pieux debout*, stakes upright.

6. "Jennings' Journal, March 8, 1766–April 6, 1766," in Alvord and Carter, *New Régime*, 176–77, citing Jennings, "Journal," *Pennsylvania Magazine of History and Biography*, 145–56. There are minor differences in spelling and punctuation between the two versions; Alvord and Carter are followed here. The "Large Colledge" that Jennings mentions was the Jesuits' residence.

7. Reyling, *Historical Kaskaskia*, 29.

8. E.g., Rocheblave to Lieutenant Governor Hamilton, March 17, 1778, translation in Seineke, *Clark*, 232; portion of a letter of Rocheblave to General Carelton, July 4, 1778, translation in Seineke, *Clark*, 257–59; MacDonald, *Lives*, 187.

9. George Rogers Clark to George Mason, November 19, 1779, in James, *Clark Papers*, 120. For a second account by Clark, see Clark to John Brown, [1791?], in James, *Clark Papers*, 208–302.

10. This interpretation disagrees with Seineke, *Clark*, xxiv, who admits that Clark maintained his hold over Kaskaskia at least in part through "braggadocio" but who nevertheless concludes that "Clark's two narratives describing these stirring days, while weird in their spelling and careless in grammar, are nonetheless convincingly honest and straightforward."

11. For Kaskaskia, in general, during this period, see Alvord, *Kaskaskia Records*.

12. Seineke, *Clark*, 594–99.

13. Alvord, *Kaskaskia Records*, 80–602; Morrissey, *Empire*, 232–34.

14. Carstens, *Fort Jefferson*.

15. Dodge's departure from Illinois for the Spanish side of the Mississippi: Anonymous, probably Father Pierre Huet de la Valinière, "Information Concerning Illinois, 1787," in Alvord, *Kaskaskia Records*, 429–31. Dodge

subsequently interferes in Illinois: John Rice Jones to Major John Hamtramck, October 29, 1789, in Alvord, *Kaskaskia Records*, 514–15.

16. Lemieux, "Huet de la Valinière"; Griffin, "Father," 203–39; Alvord, *Kaskaskia Records*, 574–80; Culemans, "Father," 339–51. This article seeks to depict La Valinière in as positive a light as possible, a difficult task.

17. Ekberg, *Colonial Ste. Genevieve*, 431, records that 135 people moved from Kaskaskia across the river to Ste. Geneviève between December 1, 1787 and December 31, 1789.

18. Alvord, *Cahokia Records*, cxliii–cxliv.

19. McDermott, "Poverty," 201. Father Gibault's lament: Rothensteiner, "Kaskaskia—Fr. Benedict Roux," 198–213, and the anonymous article, probably by Roux, "Kaskaskia," 73–79, printed in St. Louis and widely circulated in the region. See also chapter 10 of this book.

20. E.g., in 1778 the strength of the Illinois was variously reported as one hundred or three hundred warriors. Both were almost certainly wrong. Temple, *Indian Villages*, 52 and literature cited therein. The standard work on the decline of the Illinois Indians is Blasingham, "Depopulation," parts 1 and 2.

21. Alvord, *Kaskaskia Records*, 90n1.

22. MacDonald, *Lives*, 87–91.

23. For ease of identification, we consistently spell the father's name Jean-Baptiste de Couagne and the son's name Jean-Baptiste Ducoigne. Jean-Baptiste de Couagne is specifically described as the father of Ducoigne, who was the chief of the Kaskaskia in 1778: Henry Hamilton to General Frederick Haldimand, governor-in-chief of Québec, in Mason, "Haldimand Papers," 486–87. The letter is undated, but internal references indicate that it was written shortly after October 5, 1778. That chief of the Kaskaskia was certainly Jean-Baptiste Ducoigne, but Morrissey, *Empire*, 233, mistakenly calls him Louis Ducoigne. There were two Louis Ducoignes. One was born in 1750 to Jean-Baptiste de Couagne and Elisabeth-Michel Rouensa, a younger brother of Jean-Baptiste Ducoigne; he disappears from records after this baptism and probably died in his youth. The second was Louis-Jefferson Ducoigne, the son of Jean-Baptiste Ducoigne, chief of the Kaskaskia and grandson of Jean-Baptiste de Couagne, the interpreter. This Louis Ducoigne was probably born after 1781, the year Jean-Baptiste met Thomas Jefferson. Louis became the chief of the Kaskaskia after his father's death in 1811.

For the life of Jean-Baptiste de Couagne, see Graham, "Couagne," and primary sources sited therein. The Kaskaskia Manuscripts contain many citations to his doings in Illinois: 42:2:12:1; 42:6:16:1; 46:4:22:1; 46:4:22:2; 46:6:21:1; 47:1:19:1; 47:1:19:2. The citation in 48:9:15:1 also probably refers to Jean-Baptiste de Couagne but just possibly to his cousin Charles-René de Couagne, who was also active in Illinois: 50:3:14:1; 50:11:16:3; 51:1:29:1; 51:5:10:2; 51:5:17:1. The citations in 50:3:18:1; 50:4:3:2; 50:4:3:3; and 50:4:22:2 probably also refer to Charles-René de Couagne rather than Jean-Baptiste de Couagne. Faribault-Beauregard, *La population*, vol. 2, 234, and Owens, "Jean Baptiste Ducoigne," 112, citing Faribault-Beauregard, mistakenly give the name of Jean-Baptiste's father as René. After the birth of Louis, Jean-Baptiste did not remain long in Illinois. By the winter of 1750–1751, he was fraternizing with the English at Fort Edward, New York, but he still maintained communication with Canada. Both the French and English were suspicious. Jacques-Pierre de Taffanel de La Jonquière, the governor-general of Canada, ordered De Couagne's arrest, but nothing apparently came of the order. The English arrested him and a partner briefly at Albany in 1757, and he was questioned by the British commander in chief, James Abercromby, in 1758. He must have impressed Abercromby favorably. Henceforth De Couagne was employed by the British as an interpreter and confidential agent for Indian affairs. For Jean-Baptiste de Couagne as interpreter at Niagara in 1778: Henry Hamilton to General Frederick Haldimand, governor-in-chief of Québec, October 5, 1778, in Mason, "Haldimand Papers," 486–87.

De Couagne had broad experience among Indian tribes. He was captured by the Cherokee but was spared and adopted into the tribe. He lived among the Six Nations for some years and moved among the Ojibwa, Potawatomi, and Ohio River tribes as a British agent. In addition to his son by a Kaskaskia woman, he seems to have had another son by a Seneca woman. Kent and Deardorff, "John Adlum," 444n17. In 1778, Jean-Baptiste de Couagne was employed as the interpreter at Niagara, but his eyesight was failing. He soon retired to Montréal, where he was still living in 1796. My thanks to Ron Clark for help in elucidating Jean-Baptiste de Couagne's complex life.

24. Brown and Dean, *Village of Chartres*, 161 Document D-277.

25. Owens, "Jean Baptiste, 112, citing Hauser, *Ethnohistory*, 219–20. Hauser cites only the De Gannes memoir and the Raudot memoir as sources for vision quests among the Illinois. The De Gannes memoir, so called after a name on the manuscript, probably of the scribe, was actually written by Pierre-Charles Desliette, about his sojourn as a young man among the Illinois in 1688 [Desliette], "Memoire," in Pease and Werner, *French Foundations*, 352–54. But the De Gannes memoir actually contains nothing about male vision quests or name changes, discussing only female fasting and visions during menstruation. Antoine-Denis Raudot never visited Illinois. His account of the Illinois and Miami is mainly a plagiarism of Desliette's memoir with a little added material of unknown origin. Raudot, "Memoir," in Kinietz, *Indians*, 351–52, indicates only that young male "savages," tribe unspecified, went on dream quests. There is no mention of name changes, and Kinietz, *Indians*, 203–4, indicates that the Miami abandoned the practice of vision quests as

early as 1683: "There is no evidence that either boys or girls took new names." There is simply no evidence that the long-Christianized Kaskaskia practiced dream quests with consequent name changes in the mid-eighteenth century.

26. Jean-Baptiste Ducoigne gives his Indian name as "Macouissa" in the letter he dictated and gave to John Lalime, interpreter for Fort Dearborn, to be delivered to Como (more commonly spelled Gomo), chief of the Potawatomi, March 2, 1805. Carter, *Territorial Papers*, 13, 103–4. A. Levasseur, Lafayette's secretary during his tour of America in 1824–1825, gives Jean-Baptiste's Indian name as "Panisciowa." Levasseur had no knowledge of Indian languages and could not even recognize common tribal names, so his version may be inaccurate. Levasseur, *Lafayette en Amérique*, vol. 2, 311. Galbreath also confuses Jean-Baptiste Ducoigne with his son Louis-Jefferson Ducoigne. Galbreath, "Panisciowa-Jean Baptiste Ducoigne," 465–68. Many eastern tribes granted their leaders multiple titles out of respect for their various achievements and roles within the tribe. Their titles served as their names. A successful leader would have several titles, each of which served as his name depending on his function at a particular time. For example, one Choctaw chief explained that he had four names, each of which was an earned title. O'Brien, *Choctaws*, 28–29.

27. Brown and Dean, *Village of Chartres*, 161, Document D-277 and n. 1, make this succinct and insightful observation. Priests recording baptisms in this period customarily indicated that the parents were legitimately married when they believed that to be the case. Such wording is omitted here, and the priest's reference to the father is disdainful.

28. Faye, "Illinois Indians," 61, citing Thomas de Acosta to Don Luis Unzaga y Amézaga, August 29, 1775: Legajo, 2357, Papeles Procedentes de Cuba, Archive General de Indias, Seville, Spain.

29. Draper ms. 8J51: Draper's notes on an interview with Paschal Leon Carré, St. Louis, 1846, published in Seineke, *George Rogers Clark*, 540. Carré lived in Kaskaskia from 1777. He described Jean-Baptiste Ducoigne as "of small size, was unusually active, he could with greatest ease climb a smooth tree of fifty or sixty feet without a limb."

30. Stabbing at Detroit: Edward Cole to Sir William Johnson, June 23, 1766, in Alvord and Carter, *New Régime*, 320–21: "Three Illinois Indians are here (Detroit), a principal Chief, a Son of Dequones & another, they would have been with you at the Congress had not Pondiac stab'd the Chief, I hope he will recover." Although Cole records that Chief Pedigogue died in 1767, another Kaskaskia chief named Pedigogue signed a treaty in 1803, a "treaty between the United States of America and the Kaskaskia Tribe of Indians," August 13, 1803, in Kappler, *Indian Affairs*, 68. The name may have been hereditary or represented a specific role within the tribe. Ducoigne's accession

to chief: Edward Cole to George Croghan, July 3, 1767, in Alvord and Carter, *New Régime,* 580–81.

31. Faribault-Beauregard, *La population,* vol. 2, 177. A later record, Faribault-Beauregard, *La population,* 204, gives the wife's name as Hélène-Gabriel.

32. Faye, "Illinois Indians," 61–64.

33. Jean-Baptiste *fils* is otherwise unknown except for the record of Jean-Baptiste Ducoigne's burial in 1811, where "Louis et Baptiste, fils du défunt" were recorded in attendance. Faribault-Beauregard, *La population,* vol. 2, 177. Catholic Church, Diocese of Belleville (IL), *Index,* 15.

34. Faye, "Illinois Indians," 67–69.

35. Thomas Bentley to George Morgan, August 2, 1775: Bayton, Wharton, and Morgan Papers in the Pennsylvania State Archives (Manuscript Group 19), microfilm roll 5, 811–15. Seineke, *George Rogers Clark,* 34–35n7.

36. Faye, "Illinois Indians," 70.

37. Morrissey, *Empire,* 233–34, mistakenly claims that Ducoigne "secretly ... went to Ouiatenon and kept a back door open with the British" and "continued to play Hamilton and Clark against each other for advantage." Morrissey cites poorly worded, ambiguous statements in Jablow, *Illinois, Kickapoo,* 290, 293. Jablow in turn cites a letter from Henry Hamilton to General Frederick Haldimand, governor-in-chief of Québec, ca. October 5, 1778, in Mason, "Haldimand Papers," 486–87. That primary source actually reveals that far from conspiring with the British, Ducoigne brought wampum alliance belts from the American rebels to the Wabash tribes, assured them that the Americans did not covet their lands, and urged the Miami to allow the Americans free passage through their territory. Ducoigne, whom Hamilton referred to as that "bastard savage," was supporting the American rebels, not conspiring with the British.

Moreover, Morrissey erroneously refers to Ducoigne as "Louis Ducoigne" rather than Jean-Baptiste Ducoigne. Hamilton specifically refers to the Ducoigne who went to Ouiatenon as "the bastard savage son of the old man now Interpreter at Niagara, & who is chief among the Peorias." That can only be Jean-Baptiste, who was speaking for the Peoria as well as the Kaskaskia at this time. Lyman Draper's notes on his 1846 interview with Paschal Leon Carré, an old resident of Kaskaskia, includes Carré's observation that Jean-Baptiste Ducoigne "had two sons, Jefferson as he was generally called, & Battise, both now dead. Jefferson Ducoin was too young to take any part in events as early as 1781, thinks he could not have been born then." Draper ms. 8J51, in Seineke, *George Rogers Clark,* 540.

38. Galbreath, "Panisciowa-Jean Baptiste Ducoigne," 465–68. In the later part of the article, Galbreath confuses Jean-Baptiste Ducoigne with his son Louis-Jefferson Ducoigne.

39. Thomas Jefferson, "Speech to Jean Baptiste Ducoigne, [ca. 1] June 1781," in Boyd, *Papers of Thomas Jefferson*, vol. 6, 60–64; Onuf, "We Shall All Be Americans," 103–41; Owens, "Jean Baptiste Ducoigne," 109–36.

40. John Reynolds, the fourth governor of Illinois, writing in the middle of the nineteenth century, claimed that Jean-Baptiste Ducoigne had two sons, Louis and Jefferson. Reynolds, *Pioneer History*, 23. This is apparently an error. Jean-Baptiste Ducoigne's son was named Louis-Jefferson Ducoigne, generally called just Jefferson Ducoigne. Louis-Jefferson Ducoigne signed the Treaty of Edwardsville in 1818. "Treaty with the Peoria, etc., 1818," in Kappler, *Indian Affairs*, 165–66. Jean-Baptiste Ducoigne did have a second son, Jean-Baptiste *fils*, an obscure figure who appears in records only at his baptism and at his father's funeral. Reynolds wrote that Ducoigne's sons were "drunken, worthless men," which may explain the obscurity of Jean-Baptiste *fils*. Jean-Baptiste Ducoigne and Hélène-Gabriel had another child, a daughter, Marie-Ann, in 1788. She died at age four months. Faribault-Beauregard, *La population*, vol. 2, 177, 204.

4. MIXED FORTUNES, 1790–1820

1. For a recent overview of Harmar's and St. Clair's defeats, see Calloway, *Victory*; Sword, *President*; Carter, *Life*.

2. There is no adequate biography of St. Clair. Wilson, *Arthur St. Clair*, lacks citations and any critical analysis of St. Clair's career. The introduction to Smith, *St. Clair Papers*, is similarly laudatory and lacking in balance.

3. The militiamen enlisted in the War of 1812 were from Randolph and St. Clair Counties. Illinois State Archives, Illinois War of 1812 Veterans (database). For the war in Illinois in general, see Ferguson, *Illinois*.

4. Scott, *Newspapers*, 211–12; Miller, "Journalism," 149–56.

5. Davis, *Frontier Illinois*, 161.

6. Anonymous, *St. Louis Republican*, July 19, 1877, reprinted in *Fair Play* (Ste. Geneviève, MO), August 2, 1877, 2–3.

7. Account of Gustave Pape of Chester, September 27, 1913, in Burnham, "Destruction," 102–3. Pape ran a grocery and post office on the first floor and resided on the second until 1898, when he retired to Chester.

8. Similar iron ties can be seen on buildings in Charleston, South Carolina, installed after the devastating earthquake of 1886.

9. Alvord, *Illinois Country*, 404; Severns, *Prairie Justice*, 36–49.

10. Smith, *History of Southern Illinois*, 525.

11. *Combined History*, 308.

12. *Combined History*, 309, quoting a letter of November 1882 from N. C. McFarland, commissioner of the General Land Office, Washington DC.

13. The Ménard fireplace may be seen by any visitor to his home. A photograph of the Shadrach Bond fireplace, moved from his house to a location

in Evanston, is published in the Historic American Buildings Survey, https://www.loc.gov/pictures/collection/hh/index/subjects/.

14. Mason, "Kaskaskia and Its Parish Records," in Mason, ed., *Illinois*, 21–22.

15. Anonymous, *St. Louis Republican* July 19, 1877, reprinted in *Fair Play* (Ste. Geneviève, MO), August 2, 1877, 2–3.

16. Mason, "Kaskaskia and Its Parish Records," 21–22.

17. "Speech of Governor St. Clair to Jean Baptiste du Coigne, Cahokia, May 8, 1790," in Smith, *St. Clair Papers*, vol. 2, 141–44, and "Governor St. Clair to the Secretary of War, Cahokia, May 1, 1790," in Smith, *St. Clair Papers*, vol. 2, 136–40, particularly 139. St. Clair and Americans and British in general had little understanding and less regard for traditional Indian concepts of hospitality and respect. Having traveled long distances to attend a meeting, Indian ambassadors expected to be received with gifts such as new clothes to replace their travel-worn garments and other tokens appropriate for their personal status and role as tribal representatives. When these were not forthcoming, the Indians had no hesitation in reminding their remiss hosts of proper behavior. This St. Clair and others saw as begging.

18. Edmonds, "Nothing Has Been Effected," 23–35.

19. Although the Illinois population had certainly declined, specific population estimates should be regarded skeptically as rough approximations of the number of warriors at a settlement at any one time. American land speculators and settlers wanted the federal government to remove the Illinois and terminate their land claims, and depicting the Illinois as severely reduced and nearly extinct promoted that end.

20. In 1803, Secretary of State James Madison requested that Daniel Clark, a New Orleans businessman and politician, provide information about the tribes along the Mississippi. In his report, Clark describes a refugee settlement near New Madrid, on the western side the Mississippi, consisting of about five hundred Indians from six different tribes, including "Piorias," and a separate group of about thirty "Piorias Kaskaskies & Ilinois" settled among the "Whites" at Ste. Geneviève. Daniel Clark to James Madison, "An Account of the Indian Tribes in Louisiana," September 29, 1803, in Carter, *Territorial Papers*, 64.

21. William Henry Harrison to Secretary of War Henry Dearborn, July 15, 1801, in Esarey, *Messages and Letters*, vol. 1, 30. Harrison estimates that the Kaskaskia had only about fifteen or twenty warriors, which suggests a population of about a hundred. This estimation probably includes only those dwelling at Indian Kaskaskia. Other Kaskaskia were living mainly on the western side of the Mississippi among the Peoria and other tribes.

22. "A Treaty between the United States of America and the Kaskaskia Tribe of Indians," August 13, 1803, in Kappler, *Indian Affairs*, 68, where two

signers are specifically labeled "a Mitchigamian" and "a Cahokian," respectively.

23. The Illinois first ceded land for trade goods in 1773 to the Illinois Land Company, a private company of English land speculators, but the British, and then later American, governments declared the cession illegal. The Illinois also ceded land in the 1795 Treaty of Greenville, written in the aftermath of Anthony Wayne's victory over the Wabash tribes, but the Illinois were involved in the treaty only marginally and their cessions were inconsequential. The 1803 treaty is printed in Kappler, *Indian Affairs*, 67–68.

24. Potawatomi raid: Letter from Jean-Baptiste Ducoigne given to John Lalime, interpreter for Fort Dearborn, to be delivered to Como (more commonly spelled Gomo), chief of the Potawatomi, March 2, 1805, in Carter, *Territorial Papers*, vol. 13, 103–4; Edmonds, *Potawatomis*, 156–57. Kickapoo attacks: Carter, *Territorial Papers*, vol. 16, 51–52. The death of Jean-Baptiste's brother-in-law and the horse thefts were separate incidents.

25. Catholic Church, Diocese of Belleville (IL), *Index*, 15, indicates that "Baptiste Decougner, Chief of Indians" was buried on August 10, 1811. Normally, burial took place the day after death.

26. Louis-Jefferson Ducoigne signed the Treaty of Edwardsville, 1818, in first place for the Kaskaskia. "Treaty with the Peoria, etc., 1818," in Kappler, *Indian Affairs*, 165–66.

27. Kappler, *Indian Affairs*, 165–66.

5. KASKASKIA IN DECLINE, 1820–1881

1. Brandon, *Pilgrimage*, 459–60n5, indicates that Kaskaskia may not have been totally unprepared for Lafayette's visit. The *Illinois Intelligencer* of April 23, 1825, mentions that residents of Kaskaskia, Edwardsville, and Vandalia had all made some preparations in case Lafayette should happen to visit them, although it is likely that little had been done in Kaskaskia. Lafayette's announced plan was to travel overland across Illinois by way of Vandalia, and the decision to travel instead by water to save time was made in St. Louis just before the visit to Kaskaskia.

2. Levasseur, *Lafayette en Amérique*. There are a number of English translations, most recently A. Levasseur, *Lafayette in America*, translated by A. R. Hoffman. For an account of Lafayette's visit to Kaskaskia drawn both from Levasseur's account and from contemporary newspaper reports, see Brandon, *Pilgrimage*, 219–25.

3. Levasseur, *Lafayette en Amérique*, vol. 2, 299–323. Marie's father was Jean-Baptiste Ducoigne, although not mentioned by that name in Levasseur's account.

4. "Treaty with the Kaskaskia, etc., 1832," in Kappler, *Indian Affairs*, 376–77.

5. Scott, *Illinois Nation*, 40. Subsequently, the treaty of May 30, 1854, formally joined the Peoria, Kaskaskia, Piankashaw, and Wea into a single tribe known as the Confederated Peoria. "Treaty with the Kaskaskia, Peoria, etc., 1854," in Kappler, *Indian Affairs*, 636–40. Under the provisions of the omnibus treaty of February 23, 1867, most of the Confederated Peoria agreed to move from Kansas to Indian Territory, which eventually became Oklahoma. "Treaty with the Seneca, Mixed Seneca and Shawnee, Quapaw, etc., 1867," in Kappler, *Indian Affairs*, 960–69. Those who did not move lost tribal status. The Peoria Tribe of Indians of Oklahoma continues today, modern but conscious of its past.

6. Sister Josephine Barber, one of the first group of sisters to arrive at Kaskaskia, wrote an excellent account of the convent's years there, published in Troesch, "First Convent," 352–71. For a general history of the convent, both in Kaskaskia and later, see Faherty, *Deep Roots*.

7. Troesch, "First Convent," 362.

8. W. H. Crawford, "Bank of the United States and Other Banks, and the Currency, Communicated to the House of Representatives, February 24, 1820," *American State Papers*, class 3, Finance, vol. 3 (1815–1822), no. 582. This classic quotation appears in virtually every study of early Illinois banking.

9. G. W. Dowrie, *The Development of Banking in Illinois, 1817–1863* (Urbana: University of Illinois, 1913), 8.

10. For the history of The Bank of Cairo at Kaskaskia in the context of nineteenth-century banking in Illinois, see Dowrie, *Development of Banking*, 9–128; F. C. James, *The Growth of Chicago Banking*, 2 vols. (New York: Harper and Brothers, 1938); J. J. Knox, *A History of Banking in the United States* (New York: B. Rhodes and Company, 1900), 713–14, 722; F. R. Marckhoff, "Currency and Banking in Illinois before 1865," *Journal of the Illinois State Historical Society* 52, no. 3 (Autumn 1959): 365–418.

11. J. A. Haxby, *Standard Catalog of United States Obsolete Bank Notes, 1782–1866*, vol. 1 (Iola, WI: Krause Publications, 1988), 348–49.

12. The $50 and $100 notes are not listed in Haxby, *Standard Catalog*. They are apparently known only from an uncut, unsigned sheet of notes sold at auction: Stack's, Minot Collection auction, May 12, 2008, lot 3458; R. M. Smythe and Company, auction, March 28–29, 2006, lot 1699; Christie's, auction, September 14–15, 1990: Herb and Martha Schingoethe Collection; Archives of the American Bank Note Company, part of lot 1741.

13. Flagg, *Far West*, 134, 136–38, 171–74. Accounts like Flagg's formed people's opinions and may have encouraged emigration, but soberer works were also available: e.g., Peck, *New Guide*.

14. Pierre Ménard.

15. The author seems to have transposed the width of the Mississippi to the much smaller Kaskaskia, about eighty yards wide.

16. Flagg saw the old vertical-log church, which collapsed in 1838, shortly after his visit.

17. Tevebaugh, "Merchant," 270–71; *Combined History*, 308.

18. Meyer, *Meyer's Universum*.

19. Quoted in *Combined History*, 119n4.

20. *Ohio Democrat* 5, no. 47, July 18, 1844.

21. When, in 1891, William Green Eggleston sought to photograph the remains of the school and convent, all that remained was a small portion of one of the outbuildings. Brink, *Illustrated Historical Atlas*.

22. *Combined History*, 119–21. Huffstutler, *I Remember*, 24–26.

23. Brink, *Illustrated Historical Atlas*, portion of plate 25.

24. "Kaskaskia, the Old French Capital of Illinois," 125–26.

25. See chapter 10 of this book.

6. DESTRUCTION, 1881–CIRCA 1913

1. Norris, "Illinois Country," 139–52, provides an excellent analysis of the devastating effects of deforestation for the Mississippi's banks, primarily due to steamboats. Boat operators preferred woods such as mulberry, which burned hot and long, but landowners often reserved that and similar rot-resident woods for fence posts. They let loggers take trees such as cottonwoods, softer wood easy to cut and needing little or no seasoning; but such wood burns quickly, and boats had to restock more frequently than when burning firmer hardwoods.

2. Burnham, "Destruction," 100.

3. The best account of the destruction of Kaskaskia is Burnham, "Destruction," 95–112.

4. For some years the Mississippi flowed, simultaneously, in both its old channel and the channel it had taken from the Kaskaskia River, but then gradually the Mississippi shifted entirely into the Kaskaskia's bed. Currently, in dry weather the upper part of the old Mississippi River channel is a dry slough and the lower part a stream draining the River aux Vases and Saline Creek, both modest streams. At times of heavy rain and high water, the entire old course sometimes still carries water.

5. Information on the back of the photograph of Beiter's Drug Store, Missouri History Museum Library and Research Center, St. Louis.

6. E.g., Matlack, *Fair Play* (Ste. Geneviève, MO), December 30, 1893, reprinted from the *St. Louis Globe Democrat*.

7. Catherwood, *Old Kaskaskia*; Holbrook, *Old 'Kaskia Days*; Fessended, *Kaskaskia*. See also appendix A in this book for notes on photographers and sketch artists.

8. E.g., "Kaskaskia, the Old French Capital of Illinois," 125.

9. Norris, "Illinois Country," 193–201.

8. FRANCO-AMERICAN HOMES OF KASKASKIA

1. Luer and Francis, *Vanishing French Heritage*, 194–95.

2. Luer and Francis, *Vanishing French Heritage*, 195.

3. Pierre Ménard has never been subject to a full biographical study, though there are many short summaries of his life. The main holdings of Ménard's papers are with the Chicago History Museum, the Abraham Lincoln Presidential Library (formerly the Illinois State Historical Library), and the Missouri Historical Society.

4. Oglesby, "Pierre Menard," 3–19; Oglesby, *Manuel Lisa*, 65–98. The eight deaths include two Shawnee scouts.

5. Mason, "Pierre Menard Papers," 176–77.

6. Record of the burial of Pierre Ménard in the parish registry, published in Mason, "Pierre Menard Papers," 180.

7. Caton quoted in Faherty, *Deep Roots*, 359–60n9.

8. Angle, "Old Mystery," 316–17.

9. Murphy, *Lucien Bonaparte Maxwell*, 12.

10. For basic biographic information about Marie Odile Ménard and Hugh C. Maxwell, see Murphy, *Lucien Bonaparte Maxwell*, 1–19.

11. Hugh Maxwell's death is variously reported from 1832 to 1855 in genealogical sources, but the correct date is September 4, 1833: Murphy, *Lucien Bonaparte Maxwell*, 18, citing *Sangamo Journal* (Springfield), September 14, 1833.

12. Murphy, *Lucien Bonaparte Maxwell*, passim.

13. Montague, *Directory*, 39.

14. *Combined History*, 308.

15. A parallel is the John Burk slave cabin at Ste. Geneviève, although much modified over time. Luer and Francis, *Vanishing French Heritage*, 146–47.

16. Mrs. Currie was mistaken on this point. Nathaniel Pope was federal district court judge, serving from 1819 until his death in 1850, but he was not a Supreme Court judge.

17. For Jack Backus, see 1825 Illinois State Census; for John Backus, see 1860 U.S. Federal Census, household ID 2318. His reported age of ninety may not be exact. The very aged tend to overstate their ages, while the middle-aged tend to understate theirs.

9. MIDWESTERN FEDERAL AND ECLECTIC HOUSES AND THEIR OWNERS

1. Smith, *History of Southern Illinois*, vol. 1, 524.

2. The engraving appears to be made from an 1808 painting attributed to Gilbert Charles Stuart and in the possession of Bond's son late in the nineteenth century, as published in Smith, *History of Freemasonry*, 11–12, 15.

3. Exhumation of Bond's remains: *Daily Argus* (Rock Island, IL), December 3, 1879; Bond's grave: Shadrach Bond (1773–1832), Governor Bond Memorial.

4. For the construction date: Walton, *Centennial McKendree College*, 448–49. For the location on Elm Street, see *Combined History*, 306, and William Morrison's will, Genealogy.com.

5. The term *double house* indicates a house that is two rooms in width, as opposed to most houses of the time, which were just one room in width. In the manuscript, the date for the earthquake includes only the century. Presumably Sister Barber could not remember the year and so left it blank. By far the most substantial earthquakes of the region in the early nineteenth century were the New Madrid quakes of late 1811 and early 1812, which did substantial damage to Kaskaskia.

6. Troesch, "First Convent," 356.

7. For a full biography of William Morrison, see Tevebaugh, "Merchant."

8. William Morrison Ledger, Chester Public Library.

9. Tevebaugh, "Merchant," 280–85.

10. Tevebaugh, "Merchant," 270–71.

11. Tevebaugh, "Merchant," 285–90.

12. Ekberg, *French Aristocrat*.

13. Biography of Savinien St. Vrain to 1875, in *Illustrated Historical Atlas*, 46.

14. Biography of St. Vrain, in *Illustrated Historical Atlas*, 46.

15. For instance, in Bloomington, Illinois, in August 1862, a mob of soldiers and citizens, including community leaders, destroyed the office and press of the pro-southern *Times*, putting it out of business. Scott, *Newspapers*, 29.

16. For the history of the newspaper, see Scott, *Newspapers*, 51–52.

17. For the Maxwell family in general, see Murphy, *Lucien Bonaparte Maxwell*.

18. McDonough, *Combined History*, 119, 121, 126, 308.

19. *Portrait and Biographical Record*, 688–91; 1860 U.S. Federal Census, household ID 2431. The census taker's script is far from clear. The transcriber read Staley's name as Stoby, but the information recorded in the census makes it apparent that the correct form was Staley.

20. Burnham, "Destruction," 102.

21. Troesch, "First Convent," 355.

22. *Combined History*, 255.

10. "THE CURSE OF KASKASKIA"— CREATIVE FICTION, NOT HISTORY

1. The clipping is preserved in the Abraham Lincoln Presidential Library and was reprinted in an unsigned article, "Legend of the Kaskaskia Curse," *Journal of the Illinois State Historical Society*. There is no indication which newspaper originally published the story, and we have been unable to identify it. The most likely newspaper to have printed it is the *Sparta News-Plaindealer*, but no complete file of the newspaper for 1892 exists. The files of many local Illinois and Missouri newspapers are woefully incomplete.

2. 1723 census: Archives Nationales, Colonies, C13A.8.226. 1752 census: Huntington Manuscript 426, 1–7, Loudoun Collection. 1818 census: Norton, *Illinois Census Return 1810, 1818*, xxx–xxxi. The returns for Randolph County in 1810 are almost all lost. 1820 census: 1820 U.S. Federal Census, HistoryKat.

3. For the Kaskaskia clergy, see Reyling, *Historical Kaskaskia*, 35–55; Familysearch.org, Historical records collection, Kaskaskia Parish Records; Thompson, "Illinois Mission."

4. Lemieux, "Huet de la Valinière"; Griffin, "Father Peter Huet de la Valiniere," 203–39; Alvord, *Kaskaskia Records*, 574–80; Culemans, "Father de la Valiniere," 339–51.

5. Waller, "Kaskaskia Destroyed by a Curse," reprints the story from the *Jonesboro (IL) Gazette*, March 2, 1901.

6. The most widely disseminated modern account is Taylor, *Haunted Illinois*, 17–19, also online at http://www.prairieghosts.com/kaskaskia.html, and somewhat abbreviated in Taylor, *Weird Illinois*, 49–50. Other online versions include those of Supernatural Wiki, "Curse of Kaskaskia"; Ashen-AngelFox and Soul Ember, "Curse of Kaskaskia"; Iggynapster, "Kaskaskia, IL—Cursed but Not Forgotten!"; and Kuruko Darkwolf, "Curse of Kaskaskia."

7. Kaskaskia Manuscripts; Maudell, *Census Tables*; Conrad, *First Families*; Belting, *Kaskaskia*; Beauregard, *La population*, which includes Kaskaskia parish records; Tanguay, *Dictionnaire Généalogique*; Alvord, *Illinois Country*; Ekberg, *French Roots*; Montague, *Directory*.

8. Holbrook, *Old 'Kaskia Days*, 203.

9. Holbrook, *Old 'Kaskia Days*, 203.

10. Catholic Church, Diocese of Belleville (IL), *Index*, entry for July 4, 1844. St. Cyr's obituary appeared in the *Ste. Genevieve (MO) Herald*, March 3, 1883.

11. Troesch, "First Convent," 356–59. Faherty, *Deep Roots*, 14, mistakenly states that the sisters heard the story of the Indian curse, which actually appears only in a lengthy footnote in Troesch, "Reminiscences," 357–59n7, copying the Indian curse story from *Inter-Ocean* (Chicago), on February 3, 1901, and with no indication that the sisters ever heard it or any similar version.

12. Letter of October 4, 1844, quoted by Faherty, *Deep Roots*, 10, 54, 179.

13. Rothensteiner, "Kaskaskia—Fr. Benedict Roux," 198–213. Roux was the pastor in Kaskaskia from 1835 to 1839, and his memoir, first published fully by Rothensteiner in 1918, was largely derived from his conversations with the elderly of Kaskaskia. Roux testifies that the prophecy was "famous," and his memoir was used as the basis of an anonymous article, "Kaskaskia," printed in St. Louis and widely circulated in the region.

14. Mason, *Early Chicago*, 209, quotes the Draper manuscript Series W, Josiah Harman Papers, 2w124–142.

15. Montague, *Directory*, 48–49 expresses hopes for the resurgence of Kaskaskia and exhibits no anxiety about any threat from the Mississippi. J. H. Burnham was present in Ste. Geneviève in 1863 and 1867. He records that, between those two dates, the Mississippi shifted its course away from its western bank and began to scour the eastern bank toward the Kaskaskia River. Burnham, "Destruction of Kaskaskia," 100.

16. Moore, "Specimens," 723–24.

17. Washington's childhood: Weems, *History*. Moberly, Missouri: Colavito, "Lost City." Starved Rock massacre: Walcznski, *Massacre 1769*. Saucier: Snyder, "Captain John Baptiste Saucier," 217–63, exposed in Belting, *Kaskaskia*, 29n15, and Saucier and Seineke, "François Saucier," particularly 199n1.

18. *Sparta News-Plaindealer*, June 28, 1928; *Sparta News-Plaindealer*, January 26, 1962.

19. Catherwood, *Old Kaskaskia*; Holbrook, *Old 'Kaskia Days*; Fessended, *Kaskaskia*.

BIBLIOGRAPHY

MANUSCRIPT SOURCES

Alphabet Laffilard, 1627–1780: ANC D2c.222.507. Société Française du Microfilm; Reel 53: Personnel militaire et civil, Alphabet Laffilard, Colonies. Center for Louisiana Studies, University of Louisiana at Lafayette.

Archives Nationales d'Outre-Mer (formerly Archives Nationales Coloniales [ANC]). Aix-en-Provence, France.

Bayton, Wharton, and Morgan Papers (Manuscript group 19). Microfilm roll 5, 811–815. Pennsylvania State Archives, Harrisburg.

Huntington Manuscripts. Loudoun Collection. Huntington Library, San Marino, CA.

INTERNET SOURCES

1820 U.S. Federal Census. HistoryKat. www.historykat.com/IL/census/1820/census-state-illinois-1820-randolph-county.html.

1825 Illinois State Census. Randolph County Illinois Genealogy and History, Town and Township of Kaskaskia, Heads of Household. Genealogy Trails. http://genealogytrails.com/ill/randolph/1825kaskaskia.htm.

1860 U.S. Federal Census. Randolph County Illinois Genealogy Web. Post Office Kaskaskia, household ID 2318. https://randolph.illinoisgenweb.org/1860Census/1860-page312.htm.

———. Randolph County Illinois Genealogy Web. Post Office Kaskaskia, household ID 2431. https://randolph.illinoisgenweb.org/1860Census/1860-page328.htm.

American Buildings Survey. Historic American Engineering Record, Historic American Landscapes Survey. Pierre Menard House (floor plan). Library of Congress. http://www.loc.gov/pictures/collection/hh/item/il0219.sheet.00001a/.

Ashen-AngelFox and Soul Ember. "The Curse of Kaskaskia." A Study into the Supernatural, April 5, 2008. ashen-angelfox.blogspot.com/2008/04/curse-of-kaskaskia.html.

Colavito, Jason. "The 1885 Moberly, Mo., Lost City Hoax." Website. http://www.jasoncolavito.com/the-1885-moberly-lost-city-hoax.html.

Cook, Ramsey, and Réal Bélanger, eds. *Dictionary of Canadian Biography Online / Dictionnaire biographique du Canada en ligne*. Ottawa: Library and Archives Canada; Québec: Université Laval; Toronto: University of Toronto, 2003–. http://www.biographi.ca/en/bio.

Eggleston, W. G. Papers. Bancroft Library, University of California–Berkeley. A guide to the papers is available online: http://oac.cdlib.org/findaid/ark:/13030/tf3290032j/entire_text/.

Familysearch.org. Historical records collection. Kaskaskia Parish Records, First Book, p. 8. https://www.familysearch.org/ark:/61903/3:1:S3HT-6LHQ-1XS?wc=M65M YP6%3A13745501%2C14255901%2C13746703%2C14255902&cc=1388122.

Graham, Jane E. "Couagne (Du Coigne), Jean-Baptiste de." In *Dictionary of Canadian Biography*. Vol. 4., ed. Ramsey Cook and Réal Bélanger. Ottawa: Library and Archives Canada; Québec: Université Laval; Toronto: University of Toronto, 2003–. http://www.biographi.ca/en/bio/couagne_jean_baptiste_de_1720_96_4E.html.

Iggynapster. "Kaskaskia, IL—Cursed but Not Forgotten!" The Adventures of a Crazy Left-Handed Girl, January 16, 2013. iggynapster.wordpress.com/2013/01/16/ kaskaskia-il-cursed-but-not-forgotten.

Illinois State Archives. Illinois War of 1812 Veterans (database). https://www.ilsos.gov/isaveterans/war1812srch.jsp.

Kaskaskia Manuscripts, 1714–1816. Microfilm in 14 reels. Illinois State Archaeological Survey, Prairie Research Institute, University of Illinois–Urbana-Champaign. A calendar of the Kaskaskia Manuscripts, prepared by Lawrie Cena Dean and Margaret Kimball Brown, is available online: https://isas.illinois.edu/cms/one.aspx?portalId=260711&pageId=275583.

Kuruko Darkwolf. "The Curse of Kaskaskia." Blog, May 14, 2012. kurukodark.wordpress.com/2012/05/14/the-curse-of-kaskaskia.

Lemieux, L. "Huet de la Valinière, Pierre." In *Dictionary of Canadian Biography Online / Dictionnaire biographique du Canada en ligne*, ed. Ramsey Cook and Réal Bélanger. Ottawa: Library and Archives Canada; Québec: Université Laval; Toronto: University of Toronto, 2003–. http://www.biographi.ca/en/bio/huet_de_la_valiniere_pierre_5E.html.

Shadrach Bond (1773–1832). Governor Bond Memorial. State Historic Preservation Office. https://www2.illinois.gov/dnrhistoric/Experience/Sites/Southwest/Pages/Governor-Bond.aspx.

Supernatural Wiki. "Curse of Kaskaskia." www.supernaturalwiki.com /index.php?title=Curse_of_Kaskaskia.

Taylor, David. Victorian Houses. http://faculty.wcas.northwestern.edu /~infocom/scndempr/.

William Morrison Ledger. Chester Public Library. http://morrison.chester .lib.il.us/.

William Morrison's will, February 23, 1837. Transcribed by Carlene Morrison. Genealogy.com, June 29, 2011. http://www.genealogy.com/forum /surnames/topics/morrison/7289/.

PRINTED SOURCES

Alvord, Clarence Walworth. *Cahokia Records, 1778–1790*. Vol. 2; Virginia series vol. 1 of *Collections of the Illinois State Historical Library*. Springfield: Illinois State Historical Library, 1907.

———. *The Illinois Country, 1673–1818*. Vol. 1 of *The Centennial History of Illinois*. Chicago: A. C. McClurg, 1922.

———. *Kaskaskia Records, 1778–1790*. Vol. 5; Virginia series vol. 2 of *Collections of the Illinois State Historical Library*. Springfield: Illinois State Historical Library, 1909.

Alvord, Clarence Walworth, and Clarence Edwin Carter. *The New Régime, 1765–1767*. Vol. 11; British series vol. 2 of *Collections of the Illinois State Historical Library*. Springfield: Illinois State Historical Library, 1916.

Angle, Paul M. "An Old Mystery Solved: The Sculptor of the Menard Monument Identified." *Journal of the Illinois State Historical Society* 36, no. 3 (September 1943): 316–17.

Bateman, Newton, and Paul Selby, eds. *Historical Encyclopedia of Illinois*, vol. 1. Chicago: Munsell, 1918.

Beauregard, Marthe F. *La population des forts français d'Amérique (XVIIIe siècle): répertoire des baptêmes, mariages et sépultures célébrés dans les forts et les établissements français en Amériques du Nord au XVIIIe siècle*. Montréal: Éditions Bergeron, 1984.

Beckwith, H. W. "General George Roger Clark's Conquest of the Illinois." In *Collections of the Illinois State Historical Library*, vol. 1, 171–289. Springfield: H. W. Rokker, 1903.

Belting, Natalia Maree. *Kaskaskia under the French Regime*. Reprint with new foreword by Carl J. Ekberg. Carbondale: Southern Illinois University Press, 2003.

Blasingham, Emily J. "The Depopulation of the Illinois Indians." Pts. 1 and 2. *Ethnohistory* 3, no. 2 (Summer 1956): 193–224; 3, no. 4 (Autumn 1956): 361–412.

Boyd, Julian P., ed. *The Papers of Thomas Jefferson*. Vol. 6, *21 May 1781–1 March 1784*. Princeton, NJ: Princeton University Press, 1952.

Brandon, Edgar Ewing. *A Pilgrimage of Liberty: A Contemporary Account of the Triumphal Tour of General Lafayette through the Southern and Western States in 1825, as Reported by the Local Newspapers*. Athens, OH: Lawhead, 1944.

Brown, Margaret Kimball. *The Voyageur in the Illinois Country: The Fur Trade's Professional Boatman in Mid America*. St. Louis: Center for French Colonial Studies, 2002.

Brown, Margaret Kimball, and Lawrie Cena Dean. *The Village of Chartres in Colonial Illinois*. New Orleans: Polyanthos, 1977.

Burnham, J. H. "Destruction of Kaskaskia by the Mississippi River." *Transactions of the Illinois State Historical Society*, no. 29 (1914): 95–112.

Calloway, Colin G. *The Victory with No Name: The Native American Defeat of the First American Army*. Oxford: Oxford University Press, 2015.

Carstens, Kenneth Charles. *George Rogers Clark's Fort Jefferson, 1780–1781*. Westminster, MD: Heritage Books, 2009.

Carter, Clarence Edwin. *The Life and Times of Little Turtle: First Sagamore of the Wabash*. Urbana: University of Illinois Press, 1987.

———, ed. *The Territorial Papers of the United States*. Vol. 9, *The Territory of Orleans, 1803–1812*. Washington, DC: United States Government Printing Office, 1940.

———, ed. *The Territorial Papers of the United States*. Vol. 13, *The Territory of Louisiana-Missouri, 1803–1806*. Washington, DC: United States Government Printing Office, 1948.

———, ed. *The Territorial Papers of the United States*. Vol. 16, *The Territory of Illinois, 1809–1814*. Washington, DC: United States Government Printing Office, 1948.

Catherwood, Mary Hartwell. *Old Kaskaskia*. Boston: Houghton, Mifflin, 1893.

Catholic Church, Diocese of Belleville (IL). *Index to Immaculate Conception Church, Kaskaskia, Illinois*, Vol. 1: Baptisms 1692–June 1733, Apr. 1759–June 1815, and 1851–1889; Marriages 1724–Feb. 1834 and bride's index [marriages] 1834–1889 and bride's index; Burials 1721–1834, 1834–1863, 1866–1902. Belleville, IL: Belleville Diocese, 1997.

Combined History of Randolph, Monroe and Perry Counties, Illinois. Philadelphia: J. L. McDonough, 1883.

Conrad, Glenn R. *The First Families of Louisiana*. 2 vols. Baton Rouge, LA: Claitor's Pub. Division, 1970.

Culemans, J. B. "Father de la Valiniere, 'Rebel' and Illinois Missionary." *Illinois Catholic Historical Review* 1, no. 3 (January 1919): 339–51.

Czach, Marie. *A Directory of Early Illinois Photographers: A Work-in-Progress Report*. Place of publication and publisher not identified, 1977.

Davis, James Edward. *Frontier Illinois*. Bloomington: Indiana University Press, 1998.

De Berardinis, Robert, trans. "The 1752 French Census of Illinois." *Illinois State Genealogical Quarterly* 32, no. 4 (Winter 2000): 195–203.

[Desliette, Pierre-Charles]. "Memoire of De Gannes concerning the Illinois Country." In *The French Foundations, 1680–1693*, ed. Theodore Calvin Pease and Raymond C. Werner, 352–54. Vol. 23 of *Illinois Historical Collections*. Springfield: Trustees of the Illinois State Historical Library, 1934.

Diron d'Artaguiette, Bernard. "Journal of Diron d'Artaguiette, Inspector General of Louisiana, 1722–1723." Translated by Georgia Sanderlim. In *Travels in the American Colonies*, ed. Newton D. Mereness, 15–92. New York: Macmillan, 1916.

Edmonds, R. David. "'Nothing Has Been Effected': The Vincennes Treaty of 1792." *Indiana Magazine of History* 74, no. 1 (1978): 23–35.

———. *The Potawatomis: Keepers of the Fire*. Norman: University of Oklahoma Press, 1978.

Ekberg, Carl J. *Colonial Ste. Genevieve, An Adventure on the Mississippi Frontier*. Gerald, MO: Patrice Press, 1985.

———. *A French Aristocrat in the American West: The Shattered Dreams of De Lassus de Luzières*. Columbia: University of Missouri Press, 2010.

———. *French Roots in the Illinois Country: The Mississippi Frontier in Colonial Times*. Urbana: University of Illinois Press, 1998.

———. *Stealing Indian Women: Native Slavery in the Illinois Country*. Urbana: University of Illinois Press, 2010.

Ekberg, Carl J., and Sharon K. Person. *St. Louis Rising: The French Regime of Louis St. Ange de Bellerive*. Urbana: University of Illinois Press, 2015.

Ekberg, Carl J., and Anton J. Pregaldin. "Marie Rouensa-8cate8a and the Foundations of French Illinois," *Illinois Historical Journal* 84 (1991): 146–60.

Esarey, Logan, ed. *Messages and Letters of William Henry Harrison*. Vol. 1, *1800–1811*. Indianapolis: Indiana Historical Commission, 1922.

Faherty, William Barnaby. *Deep Roots and Golden Wings: One Hundred and Fifty Years with the Visitation Sisters in the Archdiocese of Saint Louis, 1833 to 1983*. St. Louis: River City, 1982.

Faribault-Beauregard, Marthe. *La population des forts français d'Amérique (XVIIIe siècle)*. Montréal: Éditions Bergeron, 1984.

Faye, Stanley. "Illinois Indians on the Lower Mississippi, 1771–1781." *Journal of the Illinois State Historical Society* 35 no. 1 (1942): 57–72.

Ferguson, Gillum. *Illinois in the War of 1812*. Urbana: University of Illinois Press, 2012.

Fessended, Laura Dayton. *Kaskaskia: A Tale of Border Warfare in Illinois.* Highland Park, IL: Canterbury, 1895.

Flagg, Edmund. *The Far West; or, a Tour beyond the Mountains.* 2 vols. New York: Harper and Brothers, 1838.

Galbreath, C. B. "Panisciowa-Jean Baptiste Ducoigne," *Ohio History Journal* 29, no. 4 (October 1920): 465–68.

Griffin, M. I. J. "Father Peter Huet de la Valiniere." *American Catholic Historical Researches*, n.s., 2, no. 1 (1906): 203–39.

Hauser, Raymond E. "An Ethnohistory of the Illinois Indian Tribe, 1673–1832." PhD diss., Northern Illinois University, 1973.

Historical and Descriptive Review of Illinois. Vol. 1, *The Southern Section.* St. Louis: John Lethem, 1894.

Holbrook, Elizabeth. *Old 'Kaskia Days: A Novel.* Chicago: Schulte, 1893.

Huffstutler, Jessie Lee. *I Remember: Early Memories of Chester, Illinois.* Chester, IL: publisher not identified, 1976.

Hutchins, Thomas. *A Topographical Description of Virginia, Pennsylvania, Maryland and North Carolina.* London: printed by the author, 1778.

An Illustrated Historical Atlas Map of Randolph County, Ills. [Edwardsville?], IL: W. R. Brink, 1875.

Jablow, Joseph. *Illinois, Kickapoo, and Potawatomi Indians.* New York: Garland, 1974.

James, James Alton, ed. *George Rogers Clark Papers, 1771–1781.* Vol. 8; Virginia series vol. 3 of *Collections of the Illinois State Historical Library.* Springfield: Illinois State Historical Library, 1912.

Jennings, John. "Journal from Fort Pitt to Fort Chartres in the Illinois Country, March–April, 1766." *Pennsylvania Magazine of History and Biography* 31, no. 2 (1907): 145–56.

Kappler, Charles J., comp. and ed. *Indian Affairs: Laws and Treaties.* Vol. 2. Washington, DC: Government Printing Office, 1904.

"Kaskaskia." *Catholic Cabinet and Chronicle of Religious Intelligence* 3, no. 1 (June 1845): 73–79.

"Kaskaskia, the Old French Capital of Illinois." *Frank Leslie's Illustrated Newspaper*, October 27, 1877, 125–26.

Kent, Donald H., and Merle H. Deardorff. "John Adlum on the Allegheny: Memoirs for the Year 1794, Part 2." *Pennsylvania Magazine of History and Biography* 84, no. 4 (October 1960): 265–81.

Kinietz, W. Vernon. *The Indians of the Western Great Lakes, 1615–1760.* Ann Arbor: University of Michigan Press, 1965.

"The Last Years of Kaskaskia." *Journal of the Illinois State Historical Society* 37, no. 3 (September 1944): 229–41.

"The Legend of the Kaskaskia Curse." *Journal of the Illinois State Historical Society* 59, no. 3 (Autumn 1966): 289–92.

Levasseur, Auguste. *Lafayette en Amérique, en 1824 et 1825; ou Journal d'un Voyage aux États-Unis.* 2 vols. Paris: Baudouin, 1829.

———. *Lafayette in America in 1824 and 1825.* Translated by A. R. Hoffman. Manchester, NH: Lafayette Press, 2006.

Lowrie, Walter, ed. *American State Papers.* Vol. 8: *Public Lands* vol. 2. Washington: Duff Green, 1834.

Lucas, Fielding, Jr., ed. *The Metropolitan Catholic Almanac and Laity's Directory for the Year of Our Lord 1839.* Baltimore: published by the author, 1838.

Luer, Jack Richard, and Jesse W. Francis. *Vanishing French Heritage: A Complete Study of the Vertical Log Homes of the Illinois Country.* Cape Girardeau, MO: Kellerman Foundation for Historic Preservation, 2014.

MacDonald, David. *Lives of Fort de Chartres: Biographies of the Commandants, Civilians, and Others from the Heart of French America, 1720–1770.* Carbondale: Southern Illinois University Press, 2016.

Mason, Edward G. *Early Chicago and Illinois.* Vol. 4 of *Chicago Historical Society's Collections.* Chicago: Fergus, 1890.

———, ed. "The Haldimand Papers." In *Michigan Pioneer and Historical Society Historical Collections.* Vol. 9, 2nd ed., 343–662. Lansing: Michigan Historical Commission, 1908.

———. *Illinois in the Eighteenth Century.* Chicago: Fergus, 1881.

———. "Kaskaskia and Its Parish Records, a Paper Read before the Chicago Historical Society, December 16, 1879." In *Illinois in the Eighteenth Century*, ed. Edward G. Mason, 1–22. Chicago: Fergus, 1881.

———, ed. "Pierre Menard Papers." In *Early Chicago and Illinois*, 162–80. Vol. 4 of *Chicago Historical Society's Collections.* Chicago: Fergus, 1890.

Matchett's Baltimore Directory. Baltimore: R. J. Matchett, 1835.

Maudell, Charles R., Jr., trans. *The Census Tables for the French Colony of Louisiana from 1699 through 1732.* Reprint, Baltimore: Clearfield, 1972.

McDermott, John Francis, ed. *Frenchmen and French Ways in the Mississippi Valley.* Urbana: University of Illinois Press, 1969.

———. "The Poverty of the Illinois French." *Journal of the Illinois State Historical Society* 27, no. 2 (July 1934): 195–201.

Mereness, Newton D. *Travels in the American Colonies.* New York: Macmillan, 1916.

Meyer, Julius. *Meyer's Universum.* Hildburghausen: Verlag des Bibliographischen Instituts, 1857.

Miller, Carl R. "Journalism in Illinois before the Thirties." *Journal of the Illinois State Historical Society* 11, no. 2 (July 1918): 149–56.

Moore, Arthur K. "Specimens of the Folktales from Some Antebellum Newspapers of Louisiana." *Louisiana Historical Quarterly* 32, no. 4 (October 1949): 723–58.

Montague, E. J. *A Directory, Business Mirror, and Historical Sketches of Randolph County*. Alton, IL: Courier Steam, 1859.

Morrissey, Robert Michael. *Empire by Collaboration: Indians, Colonists, and Governments in Colonial Illinois Country*. Philadelphia: University of Pennsylvania Press, 2015.

Murphy, Lawrence R. *Lucien Bonaparte Maxwell: Napoleon of the Southwest*. Norman: University of Oklahoma Press, 1983.

Norris, F. Terry. "The Illinois Country—Lost and Found: Assessment of the Archaeological Remains of French Settlements in the Central Mississippi River Valley, 1703–1763." PhD diss., Saint Louis University, 1997.

Norton, Margaret Cross. *Illinois Census Return 1810, 1818*. Vol. 24; Statistical series 2 of *Collections of the Illinois State Historical Library*. Springfield: Illinois State Historical Library, 1935.

O'Brien, Greg. *Choctaws in a Revolutionary Age, 1750–1830*. Lincoln: University of Nebraska Press, 2002.

Oglesby, Richard Edward. *Manuel Lisa and the Opening of the Missouri Fur Trade*. Norman: University of Oklahoma Press, 1963.

———. "Pierre Menard, Reluctant Mountain Man." *Bulletin of the Missouri Historical Society* 24, no. 1 (October 1967): 3–19.

Onuf, Peter S. "'We Shall All Be Americans': Thomas Jefferson and the Indians." *Indiana Magazine of History* 95, no. 2 (1999): 103–41.

Owens, Robert M. "Jean Baptiste Ducoigne, the Kaskaskias, and the Limits of Thomas Jefferson's Friendship." *Journal of Illinois History* 5 (2002): 109–36.

Palm, Mary Borgias. *The Jesuit Missions of the Illinois Country, 1673–1763*. Cleveland: St. Louis University, 1931.

Pease, Theodore Calvin, and Raymond C. Werner, eds. *The French Foundations, 1680–1693*. Vol. 23 of *Illinois Historical Collections*. Springfield: Trustees of the Illinois State Historical Library, 1934.

Peck, John Mason. *A New Guide for Emigrants to the West*. Boston: Gould, Kendall, and Lincoln, 1836.

Pénicaut, André Joseph. *Fleur de Lys and Calumet, Being the Pénicaut Narrative of the French Adventure in Louisiana*. Translated by Richebourg Gaillard McWilliams. Tuscaloosa: University of Alabama Press, 1953.

Pittman, Philip. *The Present State of the European Settlements on the Mississippi*. London: printed for J. Nourse, 1770.

Polk, R. L., ed. *Illinois State Gazetteer and Business Directory*. Chicago, R. L. Polk, editions 1882, 1884, 1886, and 1888.

Portrait and Biographical Record of Randolph, Jackson, Perry and Monroe Counties, Illinois. Chicago: Biographical Publishing, 1894.

Raudot, Antoine-Denis. "Memoir concerning the Different Indian Nations of North America." In *The Indians of the Western Great Lakes, 1615–1760,* ed. W. Vernon Kinietz, 339–410. Ann Arbor: University of Michigan Press, 1965.

Reynolds, John. *My Own Times.* [Belleville, IL]: [printed by B. H. Perryman and H. L. Davison], 1855.

———. *The Pioneer History of Illinois.* 2nd ed. Chicago: Fergus, 1887.

Reyling, August. *Historical Kaskaskia.* St. Louis: printed by the author, 1963.

Rothensteiner, John, ed. "Kaskaskia—Fr. Benedict Roux." *Illinois Catholic Review* 1, no. 2 (October 1918): 198–213.

Saucier, Walter J., and Kathrine Wagner Seineke. "François Saucier, Engineer of Fort de Chartres, Illinois." *Frenchmen and French Ways in the Mississippi Valley,* ed. John Francis McDermott, 199–227. Urbana: University of Illinois Press, 1969.

Scott, Franklin William. *Newspapers and Periodicals of Illinois, 1814–1878.* Rev. and enlarged ed. Vol. 6; Biographical series vol. 1 of *Collections of the Illinois State Historical Library.* Springfield: Illinois State Historical Library, 1910.

Scott, James. *The Illinois Nation: A History of the Illinois Nation of Indians from Their Discovery to the Present Day.* Streator, IL: Streator Historical Society, 1973.

Seineke, Kathrine Wagner. *The George Rogers Clark Adventure in the Illinois.* New Orleans: Polyanthos, 1981.

Severns, Roger L. *Prairie Justice: A History of Illinois Courts under French, English, and American Law.* Edited by John A. Lupton. Carbondale: Southern Illinois University Press, 2015.

Smith, George Washington. *A History of Southern Illinois.* 2 vols. Chicago: Lewis, 1912.

Smith, John Corson. *History of Freemasonry in Illinois, 1804–1829.* Chicago: Rogers and Smith, 1905.

Smith, William Henry. *The St. Clair Papers: The Life and Public Services of Arthur St. Clair.* 2 vols. Cincinnati: Robert Clarke, 1882.

Snyder, John Francis. "Captain John Baptiste Saucier at Fort Chartres in Illinois, 1751–1763." *Transactions of the Illinois State Historical Society,* no. 26 (1919): 217–63.

Sword, Wiley. *President Washington's Indian War: The Struggle for the Old Northwest, 1790–1795.* Norman: University of Oklahoma Press, 1985.

Tanguay, Cyprien. *Dictionnaire généalogique des familles canadiennes depuis la fondation de la colonie jusqu'à nos jours.* Montréal: Éditions Élysée, 1991.

Taylor, Troy. *Haunted Illinois*. 2nd ed. Alton, IL: Whitechapel Productions, 2001.

———. *Weird Illinois*. New York: Barnes and Noble, 2005.

Temple, Wayne Calhoun. *Indian Villages of the Illinois Country*. Vol. 2, pt. 2. Springfield: State of Illinois, Department of Registration and Education, Illinois State Museum, 1966.

Tevebaugh, John L. "Merchant on the Western Frontier: William Morrison of Kaskaskia, 1790–1837." PhD diss., University of Illinois, 1962.

Thompson, Joseph J. "The Illinois Mission. [Section 1] The Jesuit Successions." *Illinois Catholic Historical Review* 1, no. 1 (July 1918): 38–63.

Troesch, Helen, ed. "The First Convent in Illinois: Reminiscences of Sister Mary Josephine Barber." *Illinois Catholic Historical Review* 1, no. 3 (January 1919): 352–71.

Walcznski, Mark. *Massacre 1769: The Search for the Origin of the Legend of Starved Rock*. William L. Potter publication series, no. 10. St. Louis: Center for French Colonial Studies, 2013.

Waller, E. "Kaskaskia Destroyed by a Curse: A Tradition." *Journal of the Illinois State Historical Society* 3, no. 4 (January 1911): 67–69.

Walton, W. C. *Centennial, McKendree College, with St. Clair Country History*. Lebanon, IL: McKendree College, [1928].

Weber, J. P. *Alphabetic Catalog of the Books, Manuscripts, Maps, Pictures and Curios of the Illinois State Historical Library*. Springfield: Phillips Brothers, 1900.

Weems, Mason Locke. *A History of the Life, Death, Virtues, and Exploits of General George Washington: Faithfully Taken from Authentic Documents*. Albany: Charles R. and George Webster, [1805?].

White, Sophie. *Wild Frenchmen and Frenchified Indians: Material Culture and Race in Colonial Louisiana*. Philadelphia: University of Pennsylvania Press, 2012.

Wild, J. C., and Lewis Foulk Thomas. *The Valley of the Mississippi Illustrated in a Series of Views*. St. Louis: Chambers and Knapp, 1841.

Wilson, Frazer E. *Arthur St. Clair: Rugged Ruler of the Old Northwest*. Richmond, VA: Garrett and Massie, 1944.

INDEX

DAVID MACDONALD taught ancient history at Illinois State University for thirty-five years and in retirement has turned his attention to French colonial and Illinois history. He is the author of *Lives of Fort de Chartres: Commandants, Soldiers, and Civilians in French Illinois, 1720–1770* (Southern Illinois University Press, 2016).

RAINE WATERS is an instructor in American history, world history, and Chinese history at Heartland Community College, Normal, Illinois, and Illinois Valley Community College, Oglesby, Illinois.

 *A Shawnee Book*